COOKING
FOR
OCCASIONS

COOKING
FOR
OCCASIONS

by Maurice Moore-Betty

ILLUSTRATED BY LORRETTA TREZZO

DAVID WHITE NEW YORK

David White, Inc.
60 East 55th Street, New York, New York 10022

Printed in the United States of America

TO MY MOTHER

Who delighted in the culinary
arts, and who fostered my
life-long interest in the preparation
and serving of good food

CONTENTS

INTRODUCTION

MY INTEREST in food and its preparation dates from early childhood, and all the varied circumstances of my life have contributed to its development into a profession.

As a boy in Ireland I, with my brothers and sisters and the friends who were growing up with us, fished, trapped and later, when we were old enough to use guns, shot. We also ate the fish, birds, and rabbits so acquired. During the long weekends on the lake islands we managed our own culinary affairs. The preparation and cooking fell to me, for which I have always been thankful. The dishes thus concocted were memorable, if sometimes odd, and these meals were great adventures—a joyous release from the family table where sleeked-down hair, tidy clothes, and clean hands and faces were a must.

Interest in food was, in fact, generated by my parents. In our house a good table was always maintained. My mother was an excellent cook who therefore knew how to order meals and, when necessary, could show her cook how to prepare a dish. In her own girlhood her mother had her spend one day each week in the kitchen, preparing all the meals for the family under the eagle eye of Kate, the cook. Nowadays this kind of training is seldom possible, but it is a loss to the younger generation that girls and boys are not given some basic training in the Civilized Art. As Brillat-Savarin so wisely said, "Cookery is a science. No man is a born cook."

In the course of my life, I have lived in many parts of the world. On a tobacco farm in Southern Rhodesia, in the early 1930s, where conditions were fairly primitive, I developed a liking for fried locusts; the flavor has a striking resemblance to that of shrimp. I also made the acquaintance of maize—corn.

Later I went to the Anglo-Egyptian Sudan to grow cotton. I managed my own household and was faced for the first time with the responsibility of entertaining, though this was shared by my sister, when she came to stay for three or four months each year to escape the British winter. I had good cooks and bad, and one unforgettable master of the art. He, however, had a failing common to many cooks. He was prone to overimbibe —to calm his nerves, he said—on the days when I gave a dinner party. My solution to this was to lock him in his quarters until the afternoon and pray he would then be too occupied with preparing the meal to let his nervous system get the better of him. His shortcomings were compensated by his skills. He delighted in presenting a turkey which had been completely boned and put together again so skillfully that only adepts of the culinary art could tell. (The recipe for this rather spectacular creation, which I like to serve on Thanksgiving Day, is included in the poultry chapter.)

The canals that supplied the water to irrigate the cotton crop provided a constant supply of fresh Nile perch. The cook caught fish twice a day in a net which he threw out like an open fan. The edges were weighted with lead and the net sank to the bottom of the canal, trapping the fish. The cook was by this time up to his knees in water, his *galabia* tucked into his baggy drawers. It is hard to picture a present-day Manhattan cook in this role, even if water was accessible on which to spread the net.

Even during the years of World War II, my interest in food and its preparation never flagged. I succeeded in improvising some excellent meals in the early days of the Normandy invasion; in fact, the Colonel of the regiment was heard to say, "If you want good food, you must go to Maurice's platoon."

When the lights went on again in Europe and I settled in London, I decided the time was ripe for learning how the professionals did it. Lunching at the Ritz one day, I asked the manager if I could work in his kitchen. After I convinced him that I was serious, he pointed out quite firmly that the kitchen was the private domain of M. Avignon, who was then *chef de la cuisine*. We were introduced, and I was hired for the princely wage of $12 a week, plus laundry. It was an experience that I would not have missed for the world. The amount of sweat and training required to make a first-class chef is seldom appreciated by the layman. For this reason, when I am erroneously addressed as "chef," I make a point of denying my right to the title in the strongest terms possible.

After my training in the Ritz kitchens, I owned a small restaurant in London that provided luncheon for the boys and girls in the rag-trade district of London, near Oxford Circus. I can look back on this as an exercise in organization and management. The kitchen was about the same size as the one-sided, long, narrow space so often found in modern Manhattan apartments. We served as many as 240 luncheons in an hour and three quarters. The pace was hectic, pressure was high from noon until 2 p.m., but the experience had its lighter side. One incident I remember vividly. A good friend of mine asked if I would order canned dog food for the overpopulated kennels at her country house. As the restaurant did not run to a service entrance, all deliveries had to pass the cash desk, in full view of the seated customers, and this was the route that several cases of dog food took at 1 p.m. on one of our busiest days. The incident took a lot of laughing off, and we did not dare to serve Shepherd's Pie for several weeks.

When I came to live in the United States, it was natural for me to make food my livelihood. It was what I most like to work with, and in any case I could not raise cotton or tobacco in Manhattan—though I do garden. I have cooked for large parties and small parties, taught large grown-ups and small grown-ups. I never refer to my junior classes as children. They are much too able and too keen to learn to be placed in a different category from their seniors in years.

For many years I have been bullied, coaxed, and practically led by the nose to write a cookbook. At no time did I feel equal to the job of producing a book. I had stacks of material, but no will, and I used every excuse imaginable to keep away from the writing table. There were sowing, weeding and pruning to be done in the garden; indoors there were books to be read and new dishes to be tested. Three or four attempts having failed, I could stand the strain no longer and finally took up the pen in place of the carver and tied myself to the desk instead of the chopping block.

This book contains my recipes for the dishes I like best. These are dishes that I use when I entertain at home, have used when cooking for clients, and have taught in my school. This should be evidence that they have been fully tested.

They have been chosen among the many recipes in my collection because each dish has qualities of interest and uniqueness that make it worthy of serving, not just for a routine meal but for an occasion, whether it be a holiday, a special celebration, or that happiest of occasions, a gathering of good friends. I have always found that when I have an occasion to cook for, my mind goes blank and I turn to my collection of recipes for inspiration, finding this more convenient than thumbing through a number of cookbooks for a suitable dish. The object of this book is to provide an equally convenient source from which my readers can choose to suit their own particular occasions. Suggested menus based on recipes in the book are also included, as a convenience, since the composition of menus does not come easily to the inexperienced, and the menu for an occasion is important. I hope that the pages of this book will contribute to *many* memorable occasions.

So, good luck. Have confidence, banish fear from the kitchen and you cannot fail—at least not in your own eyes.

COOKING
FOR
OCCASIONS

APPETIZERS

APPETIZER, hors d'oeuvre, antipasto—American, French, Italian, in that order—designates the first course of the meal. In America the term hors d'oeuvre is used for the small pieces of food, which I call finger food, served with cocktails.

In this chapter appetizers and hors d'oeuvre are grouped together. Many are interchangeable and may be served either with cocktails or as the first course at the table.

Personally, and it's very personal, I rarely serve anything other than olives with cocktails when my guests are dining with me. But a straightforward cocktail party, if there is such a thing nowadays, is another matter. On these rare occasions I serve food that is on the substantial side, usually two hot and two cold foods; no dips. Many years ago when I was young, the cocktail party was exactly what it was meant to be: drinks with something to nibble on and an occasion to meet old friends and new, followed by dinner either at home or in a restaurant. This concept appears to have been mislaid or forgotten completely with the passing years. When I give a cocktail party these days I serve substantial food to sustain me and my guests through the many hours of standing, drinking, and making conversation.

An appetizer should be carefully chosen so that it in no way blunts the appetite for what is to follow.

MUSHROOMS VINAIGRETTE

Drained and served on a platter with toothpicks, these mushrooms are excellent with drinks before dinner. As a first course I like to serve them in ramekins. Marinated mushrooms are delicious both in flavor and texture, and little preparation is required. If possible, pick out those the size of a fifty-cent piece. If larger than this, halve or quarter them. They may be stored in screw-top jars in the refrigerator for several days. Save the marinade to use as a dressing for tossed salad.

> ¾ pound fresh button mushrooms
> Vinaigrette Dressing (*see page* 110)
> lettuce leaves
> finely chopped parsley

1. Cut off the stems flush with the mushroom caps and store them for another use. Wipe the caps with a damp towel.

2. Put the mushrooms and Vinaigrette Dressing in a jar with a screw top. Shake to mix. Store in the refrigerator for several hours before serving.

3. To serve, drain the mushrooms, place them on lettuce leaves, and sprinkle with finely chopped parsley.

YIELD : 6 SERVINGS

ARTICHOKES WITH MUSTARD SAUCE

> 4 artichokes
> 7 quarts water
> 1½ tablespoons salt
> Mustard Sauce (*see page* 109), 1 mixing

1. Trim the stem and small outer leaves from each artichoke. Cut about ¾ inch off the tops and cut off the tips of the outer leaves with scissors.

2. Pour the water in a large pan (not aluminum), add the salt, and bring to a boil. Add the artichokes, cover with a layer of cheesecloth, and boil for 35 minutes, or until the outside leaves pull away easily.

3. Stand the artichokes upside down on a rack to drain. When cool enough to handle, spread the outer leaves of each to expose the hairy "choke." Remove as much of this as possible with your fingers and then, with a small spoon, scrape out remaining "choke" that covers the "heart." Re-form the artichokes.

4. Serve with Mustard Sauce.

YIELD : 4 SERVINGS

CHAMPIGNONS SOUS CLOCHE

It is difficult to find a more delicious first course than mushrooms cooked and served under individual glass bells. Lacking the bells, I get exactly the same result by using an oblong pyrex dish, and sealing it securely with foil. Mushrooms prepared this way make a splendid first course to a light dinner or a main course for luncheon.

>   1 pound fresh, white mushrooms, 1½-2 inches across
>   4 center slices crusty French or Italian bread
>   6 tablespoons sweet butter
>   1½ tablespoons lemon juice
>   ½ teaspoon dried chervil
>   ½ teaspoon salt
>   ⅛ teaspoon white pepper
>   8 tablespoons heavy cream
>   4 teaspoons dry sherry
>   parsley sprigs

1. Set the oven to 375°F.

2. Remove the complete stalk from the mushrooms and put aside for another use. Wipe the caps with a damp towel.

3. Toast the slices of bread.

4. In a small mixing bowl whip together the butter, lemon juice, chervil, salt, and pepper. Spread the toast on one side generously with the butter mixture and place in a shallow baking dish.

5. Butter the mushroom caps with the remaining whipped butter mixture and arrange the caps on each piece of toast.

6. Cover each mound of mushrooms with 2 tablespoons of cream.

7. Place a heavy cover over the dish or cover tightly with foil and bake in the oven for 25 minutes.

8. Transfer the mounds to individual heated serving plates, pour a teaspoon of sherry over each, and garnish with a sprig of parsley.

YIELD : 4 .SERVINGS

COURGETTES À LA GRECQUE

You will find this combination of lightly cooked zucchini with onion and tomato purée an ideal first course for a dinner where more substantial dishes follow. As an appetizer, a small portion is best served with melba toast. For luncheon I prefer to serve it with crusty French bread with cheese and fruit to follow.

6 small zucchini squash

1 medium yellow onion

⅓ cup olive or salad oil

1 clove garlic, crushed

⅓ cup tomato purée

¼ teaspoon black pepper, or 4 or 5 twists of the mill

½ teaspoon salt

3 small tomatoes (optional)

1 tablespoon finely chopped parsley

1. Wash the zucchini, cut off ends but do not peel. Cut into ¼-inch rounds. Peel the onion and slice paper thin.

2. Heat the oil in a large, heavy skillet or saucepan. Add the onion and cook over medium heat until transparent and just beginning to take on color. Be careful not to burn.

3. Add the zucchini and remaining ingredients, except the parsley, and cook for about 8 minutes, or until the zucchini is still slightly crisp. If you wish to add the tomatoes, skin, quarter, and seed them and sauté them with the other vegetables.

4. Serve hot or cold sprinkled with parsley.

YIELD : 4 SERVINGS

VEGETABLE ANTIPASTO

This vegetable antipasto can be used in three ways. It can be served in a bowl with cocktails, or as a first course to a three-course meal. Again, it may be used as a one-dish luncheon course on the terrace in summer with lots of crusty, hot French bread. A salad is not necessary but cheese is. If you are serving it as a first course to a three-course meal, the serving should be small.

1 stalk celery

¼ pound fresh green beans

2 carrots

¼ pound small mushrooms

12 small white onions

1 small head cauliflower

2 small green peppers

1 small eggplant

1 cup olive oil

1 clove garlic, chopped

1 bay leaf

8 large green olives

12 large ripe olives

3 whole preserved red pimientos

1 cup tomato catsup

1 cup wine vinegar (French Dessaux)

4 tablespoons granulated sugar

1 tablespoon prepared mustard

salt and pepper to taste

1. Cut the celery into 1-inch pieces. Break the green beans into small pieces. Scrape the carrots and cut into 1-inch pieces. Wipe the mushrooms with a damp towel and quarter. Cut the onions into quarters. Trim the cauliflower and break into small buds. Remove pith and seeds from the green peppers and cut into thin strips. Cut the unpeeled eggplant into small cubes.

2. Heat the olive oil in a large, heavy skillet, add the garlic, and when golden remove and discard. Add the bay leaf and all the vegetables and cook over medium heat until tender but still slightly crisp.

3. Pit the olives, cut the pimientos into broad strips, and add to the vegetables. Stir in the tomato catsup, vinegar, sugar, mustard, and salt and pepper to taste and cook for another 5 minutes.

4. Cool and then chill in the refrigerator before serving. The important thing to remember when preparing this dish is to observe the undercooking rule. The whole should be *al dente*.

YIELD : 8 GENEROUS SERVINGS

PANACHE

Panache appears to have originated on the Mediterranean island of Majorca. For those fortunate enough to own an electric blender, it is a simple dish to prepare. But for the islanders it must have been a long morning's work rubbing the ingredients through a fine hair sieve. Served with drinks on a plain thin cracker, as a first course to a dinner in small quantities, or as a main course for luncheon accompanied by a salad of sliced tomatoes, you will find this "vegetable custard" an unhackneyed addition to your repertoire.

> 1 large Spanish onion
> 9–ounce package frozen green beans
> $\frac{1}{2}$ cup olive oil
> 8 ounces artichoke hearts or bottoms
> 4 eggs
> 1 green pepper
> 1 teaspoon salt
> $\frac{1}{4}$ teaspoon black pepper, or 4 or 5 twists of pepper mill
>   red pimiento and pimiento-stuffed olives for garnish

1. Set oven to 350°F.

2. Cook the beans in rapidly boiling salted water for 5 minutes. Drain and transfer to the blender.

3. Peel the onion and cut into thin slices. Heat the oil in a skillet and sauté the onion until transparent. Do not allow to brown.

4. Pour the oil and onion into the blender, add the artichokes, drained, and blend until smooth.

5. Beat the eggs to a froth in a large mixing bowl. Add the blender mixture.

6. Trim the green pepper, remove seeds and white pith, dice, and add to the bowl, mixing thoroughly. Season with salt and pepper.

7. Pour the mixture into a well-buttered, shallow, ovenproof serving dish (approximately 10 × 8 × 2 inches) and bake for 50 minutes.

8. Garnish the top with long, thin strips of red pimiento arranged in a lattice pattern with thin slices of pimiento-stuffed olives at the intersections.

9. The panache may be served hot or at room temperature. It may be prepared well in advance and kept in the refrigerator. Bring it to room temperature before serving to enhance the flavor.

YIELD : 8 GENEROUS SERVINGS

RATATOUILLE

This superb casserole of vegetables reflects the finest of the gardens of Provence. There are many variations, and slices of unpeeled zucchini may be added. This combination of alternating layers of fresh vegetables may be made well in advance and is equally delicious hot or cold. It is good on its own, served with crusty bread, followed by cheese and fruit. It provides a good standby to have in the refrigerator to serve with cold meats. It is almost impossible to give the exact amounts of vegetables required but the following quantities should serve 6 to 8 and fill a 1½- to 2-quart dish. Quantities may be reduced or increased, but bear in mind the principle of layers and seasonings.

    2 medium eggplants
    ⅓ cup olive oil
    2 large onions
    1 clove garlic
    2 red or green peppers
    3 large tomatoes
        salt, pepper, paprika to taste

1. Wash and score the unpeeled eggplants. Slice, sprinkle with salt, and place in a dish under a weighted plate for 30 minutes to remove excess moisture.

2. Set oven to 325°F.

3. Heat half the oil in a skillet. Peel the onions and slice paper thin. Peel and chop the garlic and sauté both in the hot oil until golden.

4. Trim and seed the peppers and slice. Peel the tomatoes and slice.

5. Spread a layer of sautéed onions and garlic in a 1½-quart casserole with cover. Place alternate layers of eggplant, green pepper, tomatoes, and onions, seasoning each layer lightly with salt, pepper, and paprika.

6. Pour the remainder of the oil over the vegetables, cover, and bake in the oven for 1 hour. Check the oven time carefully as overcooking will result in a purée.

YIELD : 6 TO 8 SERVINGS

CHICK PEA SALAD

Like the Vegetable Antipasto in this chapter, a small portion of this tangy and substantial salad is ideal for a first course. For summer luncheons I serve it with lots of hot crusty French or Italian bread followed by cheese (a good Fontina) and a bowl of fresh summer fruits. A chilled white or rosé wine goes well with it. This salad may be made well in advance. In fact it improves with a little keeping. Pile it on the salad greens just before serving.

> 1 can (1 pound) chick peas
> 1 clove garlic
> ½ teaspoon salt
> ½ cup tarragon vinegar
> ¼ cup olive oil or salad oil
> 1 twist of pepper mill
> ½ cup pimiento-stuffed olives, sliced
> ¼ pound Genoa salami, cut in strips
> salad greens
> 3 tablespoons finely chopped scallions or green onions
> 2 tomatoes, seeded and quartered
> 2 tablespoons finely chopped parsley

1. Drain the chick peas. Peel the garlic and crush with ¼ teaspoon of the salt.

2. Combine the vinegar, oil, garlic, remaining salt, and pepper in a mixing bowl. Add the chick peas, olives, and salami. Mix lightly and chill.

3. Line a salad bowl with salad greens. Add the chick pea mixture and garnish the top with the scallions, tomatoes, and chopped parsley.

YIELD : 6 SERVINGS

SALMON MOUSSE IN ASPIC

For a very special occasion a mousse of fresh salmon coated with aspic is an impressive beginning to a dinner party, or quite enough on its own as a main course for luncheon. Coating the inside of the mold with aspic takes a bit of time and practice but you will find the end result well worth the trouble.

> 1 cup Quick Aspic Jelly (*see page* 111)
> 1 truffle or a few black olives
> 2 cups cooked fresh salmon
> 3 tablespoons mayonnaise
> 1 teaspoon lemon juice
> $\frac{1}{4}$ teaspoon salt
> $\frac{1}{4}$ teaspoon cayenne
>   scraping of fresh nutmeg
> 1 envelope unflavored gelatin
> $\frac{1}{2}$ cup heavy cream
>   Sauce Verte (*see page* 111)

1. Place a 1-quart fish mold, if you have one, or any other shape mold you like, in the refrigerator.

2. Prepare the Aspic Jelly and cool.

3. Pour a little of the cooled aspic into the chilled mold and quickly swirl it around until the bottom and sides are well coated. Repeat until you have a layer of aspic about $\frac{1}{8}$ inch thick. Return mold to the refrigerator.

4. Slice the truffle or the olives very thin and cut into fancy shapes. Dip each piece in aspic and arrange them in a design on the aspic-coated mold. Spoon a little aspic over each one. Return the mold to the refrigerator and allow the aspic to set completely. Pour the remaining aspic into a flat dish to set completely.

5. Flake the salmon into the bowl of an electric mixer. Add the mayonnaise, lemon juice, salt, cayenne, and nutmeg and beat on high speed until smooth.

6. Soften the gelatin by sprinkling it over $\frac{1}{2}$ cup cold water. Heat very gently to dissolve, cool slightly, and add to the salmon mixture.

7. Whip the cream to soft peaks and fold into the salmon mixture.

8. Fill the chilled and prepared mold with the mousse. Refrigerate until firm.

9. To serve, run a thin knife round the edge of the mold and quickly dip the mold in hot water. Wipe the base dry and invert onto a serving platter, shaking gently to loosen the mousse. Chop the remaining aspic fine and use to decorate the platter. Serve with Sauce Verte.

YIELD : 6 TO 8 SERVINGS

LOBSTER MOUSSE

Lobster Mousse, like Salmon Mousse, makes a perfect summer luncheon entrée or, in small quantities, a rather special first course to a dinner party. As a luncheon dish, melba toast is appropriate, with a tossed green salad and a chilled white wine and a bowl of fresh fruit—a perfect combination.·

      2 cups Quick Aspic Jelly (*see page* 111)
      1 small can truffles (optional)
      $\frac{1}{2}$ cup Béchamel Sauce (*see page* 105)
      $\frac{1}{2}$ cup heavy cream
      1 teaspoon salt
      $\frac{1}{4}$ teaspoon white pepper
        pinch cayenne
   14-ounce can frozen lobster meat or 2 1$\frac{1}{2}$-pound lobsters, boiled
      1 tablespoon lemon juice
        small cooked shrimp
        parsley sprigs

1. Prepare aspic jelly and cool.

2. Place a 3-cup mold in the refrigerator until required.

3. Pour a little of the aspic into the chilled mold and swirl round, coating as much of it as possible.

4. Slice the truffles and place them in the gelatin at the bottom of the mold. Spoon a little aspic over the truffles. Allow to set and repeat the coating operation.

5. Prepare the Béchamel Sauce. In the blender combine the Béchamel Sauce, cream, remainder of the aspic, and seasonings.

6. Chop the lobster meat and add all but 2 tablespoons to the blender. Purée until smooth.

7. Stir in the lemon juice and remaining lobster meat and pour into the chilled mold. Refrigerate for several hours.

8. To serve, unmold and garnish with the cooked shrimp and sprigs of parsley.

YIELD: 6 TO 8 SERVINGS

MOUSSE OF HAM

Like the other mousses, this one is rich enough to stand on its own as a main course for luncheons, served with green beans or zucchini cooked lightly in butter, or with timbales of fresh spinach. As a first course, small portions will serve at least 8.

> 3 tablespoons finely chopped green onions or shallots
> 1 tablespoon butter
> 2 envelopes (2 tablespoons) unflavored gelatin
> 2 cups chicken stock or M.B.T.
> $\frac{1}{4}$ cup dry vermouth
> $\frac{1}{4}$ cup water
> 2 tablespoons tomato paste
> 2 cups chopped ham, tightly packed (Smithfield or Virginia is best)
> $\frac{1}{4}$ teaspoon grated nutmeg
> 3 tablespoons Madeira wine
> salt and pepper to taste
> 1 small can truffles (optional)
> 1 cup heavy cream
> watercress or parsley sprigs

1. Sauté onions or shallots in butter in a saucepan until soft but not brown. Add the chicken stock and simmer for 1 minute.

2. Sprinkle the gelatin over the combined vermouth and water to soften and stir into the chicken stock.

3. Pour about ¼ the stock mixture into the blender and purée at high speed for 1 minute. Add the tomato paste, 1⅔ cups of the ham, and the remainder of the chicken stock. Purée in the blender at low speed for 1 minute. Increase the speed to high, and purée until smooth, using a rubber spatula, if necessary, to push the mixture down to the blades.

4. Pour the purée into a mixing bowl, add the grated nutmeg and Madeira and correct the seasoning with salt and pepper. Stir in the remaining ⅓ cup ham. At this point a small can of truffles, drained and chopped, may be added for additional luxury.

5. When the mixture is cool, whip the cream to soft peaks and fold into the ham mixture. Carefully spoon the mousse into the prepared mold, and chill for at least 2 hours.

6. To serve, unmold onto a serving platter and garnish with watercress or parsley sprigs.

YIELD : 6 TO 8 SERVINGS

EGG MOUSSE

The mousse of egg is quite substantial enough in texture and rich flavor to stand on its own as a luncheon dish accompanied by a salad of crisp fresh watercress. As a first course small portions will easily serve 8.

> 1 cup Quick Aspic Jelly (*see page* 111)
> 5 hard-boiled eggs
> 3 or 4 twists of pepper mill
> 1 teaspoon salt
> ¼ teaspoon paprika
> 1 teaspoon anchovy paste
> 1 teaspoon Worcestershire sauce
> ½ pint heavy cream
>   garnish of finely chopped parsley or sprigs of watercress
>   Mayonnaise (*see page* 110)

1. Prepare the Quick Aspic Jelly and cool.

2. Shell the eggs and press the yolks through a fine sieve into a mixing bowl. Chop the egg whites rather coarsely and set aside.

3. To the egg yolks in the bowl add the pepper, salt, paprika, anchovy paste and Worcestershire sauce. Stir in the cooled aspic jelly.

4. Whip the cream to soft peaks and combine with the aspic mixture. Add the chopped egg whites and mix lightly. Chill until it thickens slightly.

5. Spoon the mousse into an oiled 1-quart mold or soufflé dish and chill for at least 2 hours.

6. Garnish with parsley or watercress and serve with freshly made Mayonnaise.

YIELD : 6 SERVINGS

CUCUMBER MOUSSE

I find this rather rich cucumber mousse a splendid choice for a luncheon, accompanied by a green salad, hot biscuits, and fruit and cheese. When served as a first course for dinner, particularly if a substantial meat course follows, the serving should be very small indeed. It also goes well with cold salmon.

> 2 whole cucumbers
> 1 envelope unflavored gelatin
> ½ cup mayonnaise
> 1 teaspoon Worcestershire sauce
>   juice of 1 lemon
>   salt and pepper to taste
> ½ cup heavy cream
>   garnish of slices of cucumber and sprigs of parsley

1. Peel the cucumbers, cut in half lengthwise, and remove the seeds. Shred the cucumbers into a mixing bowl.

2. Soften the gelatin in ¼ cup cold water and dissolve by adding ¼ cup hot water. Set aside to cool.

3. Combine the mayonnaise, Worcestershire sauce, lemon juice, and cooled gelatin. Add salt and pepper to taste.

4. Whip the cream to soft peaks and fold into the mixture. Fold in the shredded cucumber and place mixture in the refrigerator until it begins to set.

5. Spoon the mixture into a chilled 1-quart mold and chill for at least 2 hours.

6. To serve, unmold the mousse and decorate with thin slices of cucumber and sprigs of parsley.

YIELD : 6 SERVINGS

QUICHE AU CRABE

This quiche of crab is a rich combination of eggs and cream. It is versatile enough to be used as a hot hors d'oeuvre, baked in an oblong baking pan and cut into bite-size squares, or as a main-course supper or luncheon dish. I find it rather too substantial as a first course. It may be cooked in advance and reheated. If used in this way, do not refrigerate unless you plan to keep it for several days.

Basic Pastry for a 9-inch pie shell (*see page* 152)
6 eggs
$\frac{3}{4}$ cup heavy cream
$\frac{1}{2}$ teaspoon salt
dash cayenne
2 twists of pepper mill
1 teaspoon Worcestershire sauce
1 cup fresh-frozen crabmeat, shredded
$\frac{1}{4}$ cup Parmesan cheese, grated

1. Preheat oven to 350°F.

2. Line a 9-inch pie pan with Basic Pastry and bake for 15 minutes.

3. Break the eggs into a mixing bowl, pour in the cream, and beat with a whisk until thoroughly blended. Add the salt, cayenne, pepper, and Worcestershire sauce. Stir in the crabmeat and mix until it is evenly distributed.

4. Pour the mixture into the pie shell, sprinkle the surface with Parmesan cheese and bake for 30 minutes, or until golden brown and set.

YIELD : 6 TO 8 SERVINGS

QUICHE LORRAINE

Basic Pastry for a 9-inch pie shell (*see page* 152)
4 slices bacon
1 small onion
1 tablespoon butter
4 eggs
1 cup light cream
1 cup imported Gruyère or Emmenthal cheese, grated (or strong Cheddar)
salt and pepper to taste

1. Preheat oven to 350°F.

2. Line a 9-inch pie pan with Basic Pastry and bake for 15 minutes.

3. Broil the bacon until crisp and break into small pieces.

4. Peel the onion and chop finely (approximately $\frac{1}{4}$ cup). Melt the butter and sauté the onion until soft and transparent.

5. Break the eggs into a mixing bowl, beat lightly, add the cream and beat until thoroughly blended.

6. Stir in the onion, bacon, and cheese, and season to taste with salt and pepper.

7. Pour the mixture into the pie shell and bake in the oven for 35 to 40 minutes, or until golden brown on top.

8. Serve hot or at room temperature.

YIELD : 6 TO 8 SERVINGS

EGGS IN ASPIC

I have always found Eggs in Aspic a beguiling first course to a dinner party, although there are people who cannot abide the runny cold egg yolk. Lightly flavored with tarragon and attractively garnished, this dish sets just the right mood for the flavors to follow.

1 recipe Quick Aspic Jelly (*see page* 111)
1 lightly poached egg per serving
    tarragon leaves or thinly sliced truffle or pimiento-stuffed
    olives

1. Prepare Quick Aspic Jelly and cool.

2. Pour 1 tablespoon of liquid aspic into each individual ramekin or cocotte and chill until set.

3. To poach eggs: have ready a shallow pan of simmering water with 1 tablespoon of salt and 1 tablespoon of vinegar added. Roll the egg back and forth three or four times in the simmering water before breaking it into the pan. This has the effect of partly setting the white and preventing it from over-spreading. The result is a more compact and oval poached egg. Trim surplus white from poached egg to make a round or oval, according to the dish one is using. Place one poached egg in each ramekin. Chill.

4. Dip the tarragon leaves or slices of truffle or olives into the liquid aspic and arrange on top of the egg. Chill again.

5. Spoon liquid aspic over the egg to just cover and refrigerate until set.

6. Serve in the ramekin.

OEUF À LA CRÈME

Either you like eggs cooked this way or you do not. I do. There does not appear to be a lukewarm attitude. I like the combination of fresh eggs, cream, and butter. Very little seasoning is necessary and the crumbled bacon comes as a pleasant surprise. As with Eggs in Aspic, you will perhaps encounter some who cannot bear the runny yolk, in which case cook it a bit longer.

1 slice bacon per serving
2 tablespoons heavy cream per serving
1 large egg per serving
  butter
  paprika
  finely chopped parsley

1.· Set oven to 350°F.

2. Broil the bacon until crisp and crumble.

3. Lightly butter individual ramekins (½-cup size).

4. Add 1 tablespoon of cream to each ramekin, add the crumbled bacon and one egg. Cover with 1 tablespoon of cream and dot with butter.

5. Place the ramekins in a shallow baking pan in 1 inch of boiling water and bake for 15 minutes. Bake longer, if you like the yolks well set.

6. Serve hot from the oven garnished with paprika and parsley.

CHEESE PROFITEROLES

There are occasions when we must serve hot canapés and the profiterole filled with a creamy cheese mixture is by far my own favorite. I make them some time ahead and reheat them in the oven. I usually make more than I need and store them in the freezer. They keep surprisingly well. The recipe will make about 60.

Choux Paste

     1 cup water
     6 tablespoons sweet butter
     1 cup, less 1 tablespoon, sifted flour
     3 large eggs
     glaze: 1 egg beaten with 1 tablespoon water

1. Set oven to 350°F.

2. Combine the water and butter in a heavy saucepan and bring to a boil. When the butter has melted, add the flour all at once, remove from the heat, and beat vigorously until the paste comes away from the sides of the pan.

3. Transfer the paste to a large mixing bowl, add one egg and beat until completely absorbed. Repeat until all the eggs have been used. If you have an electric mixer use it with the dough-mixing arm. It takes the work out of this operation.

4. Fill a forcing bag with a plain tube half full and squeeze out mounds of paste no larger than a heaping teaspoonful onto a lightly greased

cookie sheet. Place them far enough apart to allow for doubling in size without touching and repeat until the paste is used up.

5. Brush each with glaze and bake for 50 minutes, or until puffed and golden brown. Remove from the oven to cool.

Cheese Filling

> 6 tablespoons sweet butter
> 6 tablespoons flour
> 2 cups milk, heated almost to boil
> 2 teaspoons salt
> 2 teaspoons pepper
> 8 tablespoons Parmesan cheese, grated

1. Set oven to 350°F.

2. Melt the butter in a saucepan, stir in the flour, and cook over medium heat for 3 minutes, stirring the roux constantly. Do not allow it to color. Off the fire, add the hot milk, whisking to make a smooth paste. Add the salt, pepper, and cheese, stirring until the cheese is melted. Return to the heat and cook two minutes longer, while stirring.

3. Fill the forcing bag, fitted with a small tube, half full. Pierce the underside of each profiterole and force in the cheese mixture to fill.

4. To serve, reheat in a 300°F. oven for 25 minutes.

DEVILED CRAB

Prepared in this way, deviled crab provides an opportunity for a variety of presentations—in individual ramekins or scallop shells or in a large ovenproof serving dish. A small portion is sufficient as a first course and on its own it is substantial enough for a luncheon or late supper.

> $1\frac{1}{2}$ cups Béchamel Sauce (*see page* 105)
> 2 teaspoons Worcestershire sauce
> 2 teaspoons lemon juice
>   dash Tabasco
> 1 teaspoon salt
> $\frac{1}{2}$ teaspoon dry mustard
> $\frac{1}{4}$ teaspoon white pepper

1 can (1 pound) frozen large lump crab meat (defrosted several hours before using)
2 tablespoons butter
½ cup bread crumbs, freshly grated
2 tablespoons grated Parmesan cheese
paprika
finely chopped parsley

1. Set oven to 350°F.

2. Prepare the Béchamel Sauce and season with the Worcestershire sauce, lemon juice, Tabasco, salt, mustard, and pepper.

3. Flake the crab meat and fold into the sauce. Spoon mixture into individual ramekins or scallop shells.

4. Melt the butter in a skillet. Add the bread crumbs and toss until light golden in color.

5. Sprinkle each serving with buttered crumbs, cheese, paprika, and parsley. Bake in the oven for 25 minutes.

YIELD : 6 TO 8 SERVINGS

PROFITEROLES WITH DEVILED CRAB

These large profiteroles filled with deviled crab are best served as a main course for luncheon or late supper. As a first course for a dinner party one is ample for a serving. To show it off I put it on a bed of shredded lettuce.

recipe for Choux Paste (*see page* 17)
recipe for Deviled Crab (*see page* 18)
glaze : 1 egg, 1 tablespoon water
garnish of shredded lettuce

1. Set oven to 350°F.

2. Fill a forcing bag with a plain tube half full of Choux Paste and squeeze out mounds the size of one heaping tablespoon onto a lightly greased baking sheet. Space the mounds to allow for doubling in size.

3. Beat 1 egg with 1 tablespoon of water and brush each mound.

4. Bake for 45 to 50 minutes until golden brown.

5. When the profiteroles have cooled, cut them almost in half leaving a little to act as a hinge, and fill to heaping with the Deviled Crab mixture.

6. Reheat them just before serving in a preheated oven (350°F.) for 25 minutes. Serve them on a bed of shredded lettuce.

CREAMED SMOKED HADDOCK

The lavish use of seasonings sometimes destroys the distinctive character of foods. Smoked haddock has its own very individual flavor. In this recipe I use a little fresh lemon juice, which serves to emphasize rather than blanket the smoky flavor of the fish. I have included this with appetizers but this recipe will serve 4 generously as a first course, or as a main course for a luncheon. The entire recipe may be made in advance, even refrigerated, and then reheated before serving until it begins to bubble. It also freezes well.

> 1–pound piece of smoked haddock (about $1\frac{3}{4}$ cups, boned)
> 1 cup milk
> $\frac{1}{2}$ cup water
> $2\frac{1}{2}$ tablespoons sweet butter
> 2 tablespoons flour
> 1 cup fish liquid
> 3 or 4 twists of pepper mill
> dash cayenne
> 1 teaspoon lemon juice
> Topping: 2 tablespoons sweet butter
> 3 tablespoons bread crumbs, freshly grated
> 4 rectangles cut from slices of bread
> garnish of finely chopped parsley

1. Set oven to 450°F.

2. Place the haddock in a saucepan, pour in the milk and water, bring to a simmer, and cook for 6 to 8 minutes or until the fish flakes easily, being careful not to allow it to boil over.

3. Drain the haddock, reserving the liquid, and when cool enough to handle, remove the skin and bones.

4. Melt the butter in a saucepan, stir in the flour, and cook for 3 minutes. Add the fish liquid and whisk till smooth. Season with pepper, cayenne, and lemon juice and mix with the cooked smoked haddock.

5. Fill 4 scallop shells with the mixture. (Ramekins may also be used.)

6. For the topping, melt the butter and stir in the bread crumbs until they are thoroughly coated. Spread the bread crumbs over the haddock evenly to the very edges of the shells.

7. If scallop shells are used, cut four rectangles of bread and place them on a baking sheet. The bread will keep the scallop shells horizontal. Place the filled shells on top and bake for 10 minutes.

8. To serve, place the shell and underlayer of bread on individual serving dishes and sprinkle lightly with parsley.

YIELD : 4 SERVINGS

SMOKED SALMON

Smoked salmon is, in my opinion, much too expensive and delicious to do anything to it other than slice it paper thin—and it *must* be thinly sliced—and serve it with buttered brown bread and a wedge of lemon.

When ordering smoked salmon take special care that it *is* sliced very thin. The smoked salmon from Nova Scotia and Norway are of excellent quality but I don't really think anything can equal the flavor of smoked salmon from Scotland. Too often smoked salmon is served with onions, capers, and sauces. These are not at all necessary.

FRESH CAVIAR

The less one does to fresh caviar and the more said about it the better. Like smoked salmon, it is a luxury and needs nothing more than a wedge of lemon tied in a piece of cheesecloth so that one may add a few drops of juice without any seeds or pulp. All too often it is served with chopped onion, egg, or sour cream but these additions are an insult to this great food.

SMOKED TROUT

Trout is another of the finest of smoked fish and makes an excellent first course or light luncheon dish, though not a very slimming one. Serve half a large trout or a small whole trout for each person, with lightly buttered brown bread, and fresh horseradish sauce. Follow this with a salad, cheese, and a bowl of fresh fruit to make a perfect summer meal on the terrace.

SOUPS

SOUP is delicious, nourishing and useful. It need not be fattening, as many people have been led to believe. Cream of vegetable soup, without cream, has approximately 9 calories per cup. For luncheon, with a slice of toast or a cracker, it is in my opinion preferable to a sandwich and a cup of coffee, and much better for one. I attempt to keep white and brown stock in my freezer to use as bases for endless varieties of soups and consommés. In this chapter you will find instructions for preparing White Stock, Brown Stock, and Double Consommé. A cup of consommé at any time of the day is a hunger breaker, and can quickly take the place of the cup of coffee or tea. A meal begun with a cup of consommé is sure to be a success. The gastric juices begin to flow right away.

When I make a large quantity of soup I freeze it in a rather thin block by leaving the soup in the bottom of a large pan. I remove the block and cut it into wedges which are promptly wrapped in foil and stored in the freezer for future use.

In making cream of vegetable soups, I use approximately 3 cups of stock, white or brown, to 2 packed cups of diced vegetables. You may use more or less depending on the vegetables. The vegetables are cooked in a little stock till tender; this mixture is puréed in the blender and then added to the remaining stock. You can substitute more stock for some or all of the cream, if desired. These are simple soups to prepare and when properly garnished look beautiful. You will find examples and combinations in this chapter. Read them and use your imagination to devise others. You will be amazed at the results, and so will your guests.

DOUBLE CONSOMMÉ

2 quarts Brown Stock (*see foot of page*)
1 onion, coarsely chopped
1 stick celery, chopped
1 carrot, scraped, chopped
2 egg whites
  crushed shells of 2 eggs
½ pound shin of beef, ground
1 bay leaf
1 sprig thyme (½ teaspoon dried)
1 sprig marjoram (½ teaspoon dried)
2 cloves
12 peppercorns
¼ cup dry sherry
2 teaspoons sugar
  salt to taste

1. If stock has been chilled, remove all the fat. Pour the stock into a large saucepan. Add the vegetables.

2. Whip the egg whites, and add the crushed shells. Combine with the ground meat, and add 1 tablespoon cold water.

3. Add the meat and egg mixture to the stock. Add the herbs and spices. Whisk the mixture over medium heat until it comes to a boil, lower the heat and simmer for 10 minutes. Add the sherry. Bring to a boil once more and then remove from the heat. Let it stand for 5 minutes.

4. Strain the soup through 4 or 5 thicknesses of cheesecloth. Return to the pan; add sugar and salt to taste.

5. To serve, reheat, or, if you plan to serve it cold, chill thoroughly and garnish each serving with a thin slice of lemon.

BROWN STOCK (BEEF STOCK)

½ cup salad oil
1 stalk celery, coarsely chopped
2 onions
2 carrots

    2 leeks (if available), washed and chopped
    1 small white turnip (if available), chopped
    2 pounds knuckle of veal, chopped coarsely, with bones, cracked
    4 pounds shin of beef, cut in chunks
    2 cups chicken giblets: gizzards, necks, but on no account livers
        bouquet garni
    6 quarts water

1. Heat the oil in a large, heavy saucepan. Add the vegetables and veal bones and brown thoroughly.

2. Add the beef, veal, and chicken giblets, and the bouquet garni. Pour in the water and bring slowly to a boil.

3. As scum rises, skim carefully. Simmer very gently for 5 hours.

4. Strain, and when stock is cool, store it in the freezer.

WHITE STOCK

Stock is useful to have in your freezer. Make several quarts at a time. It is the base for many soups, sauces, and gravies. Vegetables cooked in it are improved beyond recognition.

     4 pounds knuckle of veal (or veal shank)
        bones of poultry, if available
     6 quarts water
     2 onions, stuck with 2 cloves
     2 carrots, chopped
     2 leeks, washed thoroughly
     1 rib of celery, chopped
    12 peppercorns
     1 tablespoon salt
        bouquet garni (parsley, thyme and bay leaf)

1. Ask your butcher to chop the meat and bones into large pieces. Place them in a large saucepan, add 6 quarts of water, and bring slowly to a boil. Remove the scum as it rises. From time to time, add a little cold water as this will help the scum rise to the top.

2. When the scum has been removed, and no longer forms, add the vegetables, peppercorns, salt, and bouquet garni. Simmer over very low heat for 5 hours. Strain the stock into a large bowl and chill. Remove every particle of fat.

CREAM OF ARTICHOKE SOUP

> 2 cups artichoke bottoms or hearts, drained
> 1 small onion, chopped
> 4 cups chicken stock
> 3 tablespoons sweet butter
> 2 tablespoons flour
> 1 cup light cream
> salt and pepper to taste
> finely chopped parsley

1. Combine the artichokes, onion, and stock in a saucepan and simmer, covered, for 15 minutes.

2. Pour the contents into the blender and purée, or press through a fine sieve.

3. Melt the butter in the saucepan, add the flour, and cook for 3 minutes, stirring constantly. Stir in the purée, bring to a boil, and cook for 3 minutes.

4. Remove from the fire, add the cream, and season with salt and pepper. The cream may be omitted, and stock added to thin the soup to the desired consistency.

5. To serve, reheat and serve with a sprinkling of parsley.

YIELD : 8 SERVINGS

CREAM OF CARROT SOUP

> 6 medium carrots, scraped, chopped
> 1 small onion, peeled, chopped
> 1 bay leaf
> 2 cups chicken stock
> 3 tablespoons sweet butter

    2 tablespoons flour
    1 cup light cream
      salt and pepper to taste
      garnish : finely chopped parsley and grated lemon rind

1. In a saucepan combine the carrots, onion, bay leaf, and stock and simmer, covered, for 20 minutes.

2. Pour the contents into the blender and purée, or press through a fine sieve.

3. Melt the butter in the saucepan, add the flour and cook for 3 minutes, stirring constantly. Stir in the purée, bring to a boil and cook for 3 minutes.

4. Remove from the fire, add the cream, and season with salt and pepper.

5. Serve hot with a sprinkling of parsley and grated lemon rind.

YIELD : 4 TO 6 SERVINGS

CREAM OF CELERY SOUP

    3 cups finely chopped celery
    1 small onion, chopped
    1 bay leaf
    3 cups chicken stock
    3 tablespoons sweet butter
    2 tablespoons flour
    1 cup light cream
    $\frac{1}{2}$ teaspoon imported curry powder
      salt and pepper to taste
      garnish of finely chopped parsley

1. In a saucepan combine the celery, onion, bay leaf, and stock and simmer, covered, for 20 minutes.

2. Pour the contents of the saucepan into the blender and purée, or press through a fine sieve.

3. Melt the butter in the saucepan, add the flour, and cook for 3 minutes, stirring constantly. Stir in the purée, bring to a boil, and cook for 3 minutes.

4. Remove from the fire and add the cream, curry powder, salt and pepper. Reheat, being careful not to allow the soup to boil.

5. Serve hot with a sprinkling of parsley.

YIELD : 6 TO 8 SERVINGS

CREAM OF SPINACH SOUP

1 9-ounce package frozen spinach, chopped or leaf
1 small onion, finely chopped
3 cups chicken stock
3 tablespoons sweet butter
2 tablespoons flour
1 cup light cream
¼ teaspoon freshly grated nutmeg
salt and pepper to taste
finely chopped parsley

1. In a saucepan combine the spinach, onion, and chicken stock and simmer, covered, for 10 minutes.

2. Pour the contents of the saucepan into blender and purée, or press through a fine sieve.

3. Melt the butter in the saucepan, add the flour and cook for 3 minutes, stirring constantly. Stir in the purée, bring to a boil and cook for 3 minutes.

4. Remove from the fire. Add the cream and season with nutmeg, salt and pepper. As in other cream of vegetable soups, cream may be left out and a little extra stock added.

5. To serve, reheat and serve hot with a sprinkling of parsley.

YIELD : 6 TO 8 SERVINGS

COLD TOMATO CONSOMMÉ

    2 cups canned Italian plum tomatoes with basil
    4 cups chicken stock
    1 tablespoon sugar
    ¼ cup dry vermouth
      salt and pepper to taste
      garnish of finely chopped parsley or shredded lemon rind

1. Combine the tomatoes and chicken stock in a saucepan, bring to a boil, and simmer for 5 minutes.

2. Rub the soup through a fine sieve into another saucepan. Add the sugar and vermouth and season with salt and pepper.

3. Serve hot or cold with a garnish of parsley or lemon rind. If you have fresh basil, add a little of it, chopped fine, with the parsley or lemon rind.

YIELD : 6 TO 8 SERVINGS

ICED CUCUMBER SOUP

    2 cucumbers
    ½ cup finely chopped onion
    3 cups chicken stock
    1 cup sour cream
    1 tablespoon finely chopped parsley
    ½ teaspoon fresh dill, finely chopped (or ¼ teaspoon dried)
      salt and pepper to taste

1. Peel 1 cucumber, cut it lengthwise, and remove the seeds. Dice cucumber and place it in a saucepan. Add the onion and chicken stock and simmer, covered, for 20 minutes.

2. Pour the mixture into the blender and purée, or press through a fine sieve into a mixing bowl.

3. Peel the other cucumber, remove seeds, and grate cucumber into the puréed mixture. Stir in the sour cream, parsley, and dill. Season to taste with salt and pepper.

4. Chill thoroughly before serving.

YIELD : 6 TO 8 SERVINGS

CHILLED VEGETABLE SOUP

This soup is at its best if allowed to stand in the refrigerator for 8 hours before serving, but it can also be successfully made and served in less time by adding ice cubes to chill. The quantities given here are guides. If you prefer more tomato, by all means put it in, or omit the green pepper, if desired.

> 3 medium (ripe) tomatoes
> 3 tablespoons olive oil
> 3 tablespoons red wine vinegar
> 1 clove garlic, chopped
> 2 cups chicken stock
> $\frac{1}{2}$ medium cucumber
> 1 small green pepper
> 3 tablespoons finely chopped green onions
>   dash Tabasco sauce
>   salt and pepper to taste
> 1 tablespoon sugar
> 1 tablespoon finely chopped parsley

1. Dip tomatoes into boiling water for 1 minute to loosen the skins. Peel the tomatoes, remove seeds, and chop.

2. Put the chopped tomatoes into the blender, add the olive oil, vinegar, garlic, and enough chicken stock to cover. Blend until smooth. Pour the mixture into a bowl and stir in the remaining chicken stock.

3. Peel the cucumber, cut in half, remove seeds, chop fine, and add to the soup.

4. Cut the green pepper in half, remove·seeds and cut away white pith. Chop fine and add to the soup.

5. Add the green onions, Tabasco sauce, salt, pepper, and sugar and mix well.

6. Serve well chilled and garnished with a sprinkling of finely chopped parsley.

YIELD : 4 TO 6 SERVINGS

LOW-CALORIE VEGETABLE SOUP

> 1 tablespoon butter
> 3 medium carrots, scraped and diced
> 2 stalks celery, washed and diced
> 1 small onion, diced
> 1 quart chicken stock
> $\frac{1}{4}$ teaspoon celery salt
> $\frac{1}{2}$ teaspoon salt
> 2 or 3 twists of pepper mill
> $\frac{1}{4}$ cup dry vermouth
> 1 tablespoon sugar
> finely chopped parsley

1. Melt the butter in a heavy saucepan, add three quarters of the diced vegetables, cover the saucepan, and cook over low heat for 10 minutes.

2. Put the vegetables in the blender, add a little of the chicken stock, and purée. Return puréed mixture to the saucepan.

3. Add the remainder of the chicken stock, seasonings, and remaining vegetables. Bring to a boil, lower heat, and simmer for 5 minutes.

4. Serve hot with a sprinkling of chopped parsley.

YIELD : 6 SERVINGS

PEANUT SOUP

I first came across this soup when I lived in the Sudan. It was almost the only soup known to the local cooks, and one got so one couldn't stand the sight of it. Now, after many years away from that strange country, and not being confronted with "fool Soudani" three or four times a week, I love it. If you have a liking for the taste of peanuts you will love it, too.

    ½ cup shelled unsalted peanuts

    3 cups beef or chicken stock

    ½ teaspoon chili powder

    ½ teaspoon salt

    1 cup milk

1. Purée the nuts and stock in the blender until smooth.

2. Pour the mixture into a saucepan; add the chili powder and salt. Cook over low heat for 15 minutes. Stir in the milk.

3. This may be served either hot or cold. To serve hot, garnish with a tablespoon of heavy cream in each plate and a sprinkle of finely chopped parsley. If the soup is to be served cold, chill in the refrigerator and garnish with paper-thin slices of cucumber and radish.

YIELD : 4 SERVINGS

OYSTERS ESPAGNOL

When I first served oysters in this fashion it was not as a soup but as a fish course. I serve it as a soup and find it delicious for luncheon, with toast or biscuits.

    24 oysters in their shells or 1 quart shelled oysters

    3 tablespoons sweet butter

    ¼ cup white wine

    ¼ cup oyster liquid

    ½ cup Brown Sauce (*see page* 107)

    3 or 4 twists of pepper mill

    1 tablespoon lemon juice

    ½ tablespoon finely chopped parsley
       triangles of dry toast

1. If oysters are in their shells, open them, remove the beards, detach oysters and reserve the liquid.

2. Combine the oysters, butter, wine, and oyster liquid in a saucepan, and cook for 2 minutes over medium heat.

3. Add the Brown Sauce, pepper, and lemon juice, and heat through just before serving.

4. Pour into large soup bowls, garnish with parsley, and serve with triangles of toast.

YIELD : 2 SERVINGS

SALADS

MANY of the salads for which recipes are given here I serve as a first course. The ones that I usually serve this way are Niçoise, Marguery, Asparagus and Avocado, Romano, Cauliflower and Beet, and sometimes Spinach Salad. The Winter Salad I usually include in a buffet because of its staying power. Unlike the delicate green salads, it contains nothing that will wilt. Green Salad, served in the middle of the meal, perhaps with cheese, should be made of Boston, Bibb, or romaine lettuce with Vinaigrette Dressing.

Brillat-Savarin remarks, "Salad refreshes without weakening and comforts without irritating." What more could one ask for?

GREEN SALAD

Choose your greens carefully. One can be fooled by a head of lettuce. My favorites for Green Salad are Boston, Bibb, or romaine lettuce. Iceberg, salad bowl, and field lettuce, chicory and escarole are other favorite greens.

Wash greens and dry them thoroughly. Keep in the refrigerator until you are ready to make the salad. Tear, don't cut, into manageable-sized pieces in a salad bowl. Add dressing and toss just before serving. I always serve Green Salad with Vinaigrette Dressing (*see page* 110).

35

SALADE NICOISE

       lettuce leaves
1 can tuna fish (6 ounces)
1 cup shredded ham or chicken, or small whole shrimp
½ pound assorted cooked vegetables (green beans, peas, zucchini, artichokes, etc.)
½ cucumber, sliced
1 teaspoon each chopped fresh herbs (parsley, tarragon, basil, etc.)
1 pound tomatoes
1 can anchovy filets, drained
12 black olives
1 recipe Vinaigrette Dressing (*see page* 110)

1. Line a salad bowl with lettuce leaves. Drain and flake the tuna, and place in the bowl. Add the ham, chicken, or shrimp, the cooked vegetables, and cucumber. Sprinkle with the herbs.

2. Peel, seed, and slice the tomatoes. Arrange the slices over the vegetables, and garnish with anchovies and olives. Add the Vinaigrette Dressing just before serving.

YIELD : 6 SERVINGS

SALAD MARGUERY

       lettuce leaves
3 hard-boiled eggs
¼ pound cooked shrimp
1 cup thinly sliced dill pickle
4 to 6 tomatoes
       butter
1 can anchovy filets, drained
1 mixing Vinaigrette Dressing (*see page* 110)
2 tablespoons tomato catsup

1. Line a salad bowl with lettuce leaves.

2. Remove the yolks from the eggs and press through a fine sieve. Cut the white into thin strips and place them on the lettuce. Scatter the

shrimp on top, and sprinkle with the sieved egg yolk. Cover with the dill pickle.

3. Peel the tomatoes, cut them in half, and sauté very lightly in a little butter. Arrange them on top of the salad mixture, cut side down.

4. Cut the anchovy filets in half lengthwise and arrange them on top of the tomatoes in a lattice pattern.

5. Combine the Vinaigrette Dressing and tomato catsup, and spoon over the salad just before serving.

YIELD : 6 SERVINGS

SALAD ROMANO

I usually serve this as a first course. It has an awful lot of character, and is inclined to overwhelm the parent dish if served as an accompaniment.

$\frac{1}{4}$ pound Gruyère cheese
3 ribs celery
3 or 4 medium mushrooms
1 tablespoon finely chopped parsley
1 mixing Vinaigrette Dressing (*see page* 110)

1. Slice the cheese very thin and cut into julienne strips about $1\frac{1}{2}$ inches long. Wash the celery and scrape it, if necessary. Cut across the ribs into sections $1\frac{1}{2}$ inches long, and then cut into thin julienne strips. Wipe the mushrooms with a damp cloth and slice very thin.

2. Combine all ingredients in a salad bowl and toss lightly. Allow to stand for 15 to 20 minutes.

YIELD : 4 TO 6 SERVINGS

ASPARAGUS AND AVOCADO SALAD

I have listed this under salads for want of a better place. Like Salad Romano, it is too hearty to be served as an accompaniment. With fresh, crisp Italian or French bread it makes an adequate luncheon dish, and may be followed by a ripe Brie.

2 bunches fresh asparagus (approx. 2 pounds)
1 avocado (not too ripe)
½ cup Vinagrette Dressing (*see page* 110)
6 to 8 radishes
   lettuce leaves
2 tablespoons finely chopped parsley

1. Scrape the asparagus stalks with a vegetable peeler, and cut off the white ends, if tough. Cut off the tips and set aside. Cut the stalks on the bias into 1-inch pieces.

2. Bring a saucepan of salted water to a boil. Place the tips in water for 2 minutes of boiling time. Remove and drain. Add the stalks for 4 minutes of boiling time. Remove and drain.

3. Peel the avocado, cut into 2-inch cubes, and place in a salad bowl. Pour over the Vinaigrette Dressing immediately to prevent discoloration.

4. Trim the radishes, slice very thinly, and cut into julienne strips. Add to the avocado. Add the cooled asparagus pieces and toss lightly.

5. To serve, pile the mixture onto lettuce leaves and sprinkle with parsley.

YIELD : 4 TO 6 SERVINGS

CAULIFLOWER AND BEET SALAD

1 small cauliflower
½ cup young cooked beets, diced or cut in strips
½ tablespoon finely chopped green onion
2 tablespoons finely chopped parsley
   your favorite oil and vinegar dressing

1. Trim the cauliflower into bite-size flowerettes and soak for 10 minutes in cold salted water. Bring 3 quarts of water to a boil, add 3 tablespoons salt, and cook the cauliflower buds for 5 or 6 minutes. Test them; they should be slightly underdone. Drain and cool.

2. Place the cauliflower in a salad bowl, add the beets, green onion, parsley, and dressing. Toss lightly. This salad improves if allowed to stand for an hour at room temperature before serving.

YIELD : 4 TO 6 SERVINGS

ENDIVE AND BEET SALAD

    1 pound fresh Belgian endive
    ½ cup cooked beets, cut in julienne slices
      Vinaigrette Dressing (*see page* 110)
    1 tablespoon finely chopped parsley

1. Wash the endive thoroughly and slice on the bias. Drain and mix with the beets in a salad bowl.

2. Add Vinaigrette Dressing and toss lightly. Sprinkle with finely chopped parsley just before serving.

SPINACH SALAD

    Dressing
    1 egg
    2 teaspoons Parmesan cheese
    2 tablespoons Dijon mustard
      juice of 1 lemon
    1 teaspoon sugar
    1 teaspoon Worcestershire sauce
    ¼ cup salad oil
      salt and pepper to taste

    Salad
    1 pound fresh spinach
    6 slices bacon, grilled, crumbled
    2 hard-boiled eggs

1. In a mixing bowl combine the raw egg, cheese, mustard, lemon juice, sugar, and Worcestershire sauce. Mix thoroughly, add the oil, and mix again. Season with salt and pepper.

2. Pick over the spinach, using only the crisp, fresh tops. Wash the spinach thoroughly in several changes of water. Drain until the leaves are free of water.

3. Just before serving, place the spinach leaves in a salad bowl. Sprinkle the bacon crumbs over the spinach. Chop the eggs and add. Pour the dressing over the leaves and toss until all the ingredients are thoroughly coated.

YIELD : 6 SERVINGS

WINTER SALAD

When I entertain *à la fourchette,* this solves the salad problem. It looks and tastes just as good an hour after it has been assembled, unlike the green salad that reminds me of wet tissue after a short period of waiting.

> 2 9-ounce packages frozen whole green beans
> 1 medium red onion
> 2 small ribs celery
> 1 medium green pepper
> 4 or 5 radishes
>   your favorite oil and vinegar dressing
>   lettuce leaves
> 2 medium tomatoes
> 2 tablespoons finely chopped parsley

1. Defrost the beans and cook them in boiling salted water for 5 minutes. Drain.

2. Peel the onion and slice very thin. Dice the celery. Cut the pepper in half, remove the seeds and white pith, and cut into thin strips. Wash and trim the radishes and cut into thin rounds. Combine the vegetables in a bowl, pour the dressing over them, and mix well. Allow to stand for an hour or so.

3. Line a salad bowl with lettuce leaves and fill with the vegetable mixture. Peel and quarter the tomatoes and place around the edge. Sprinkle with finely chopped parsley.

YIELD : 6 TO 8 SERVINGS

POTATO SALAD

> 2½ to 3 pounds "old" medium-sized potatoes
> 1 small yellow onion

½ small green pepper
3 tablespoons finely chopped parsley
1 mixing Vinaigrette Dressing (*see page* 110)
2 tablespoons mayonnaise
lettuce leaves

1. Cook the potatoes in their skins in boiling water until firm, but do not overcook.

2. Peel the onion and chop fine. Remove seeds and white pith from the green pepper and chop fine. Combine the onion, pepper, and parsley in a bowl.

3. While the potatoes are still hot, peel, dice, and add to the bowl. Mix together the Vinaigrette Dressing and mayonnaise and pour over the salad immediately. Toss lightly, and allow to stand for at least one hour.

4. Line a salad bowl with lettuce leaves and pile the potato salad in the center.

YIELD : 6 TO 8 SERVINGS

LOBSTER SALAD

2 1½-pound boiled lobsters or 1 pound fresh-frozen lobster
1 cup finely diced celery
2 tablespoons finely chopped parsley
lettuce leaves
1 egg yolk
Vinaigrette Dressing (*see page* 110)

1. If freshly boiled lobster is used, remove all the meat from the shell. Cut tail portions into chunks. Reserve some of the claw portions for garnish. If fresh-frozen lobster is used, drain, remove cartilage and cut up into large pieces.

2. Mix lobster meat with celery and parsley.

3. Line a salad bowl with lettuce leaves, and pile the lobster on top. Garnish with reserved claw portions.

4. Beat egg yolk into the Vinaigrette Dressing, pour over the lobster, and serve.

YIELD : 4 SERVINGS

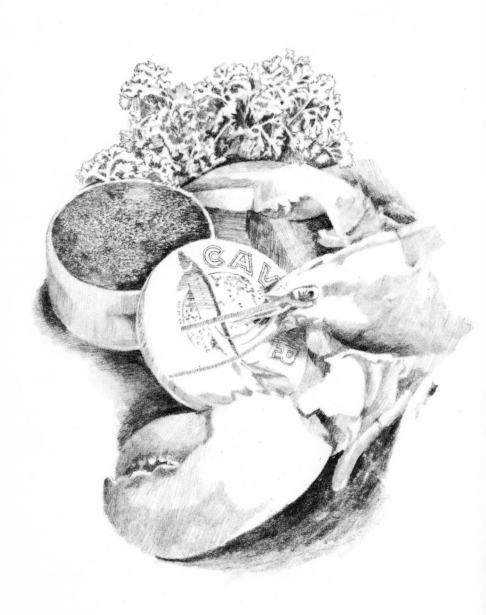

FISH AND SHELLFISH

LOOKING back there were few fishless periods in my life. The only one that I can really remember was during active service in World War II. One highlight of my army career was when I was ordered (one was never asked) to undertake a gastronomic mission. The Regiment was entertaining Viscount Montgomery at luncheon and as the colonel's aide I was detailed to find a supply of fresh oysters. I scoured the lowlands and came up with more than enough for his lordship and me. It is virtually impossible to be more than 50 miles from the sea if one lives in the British Isles, and there are numerous fresh-water sources of fish almost everywhere.

In my young days I cannot ever remember being told to eat fish because it was high protein and therefore good for me. I ate it because I liked it. Salmon was plentiful when in season, and in those days things were in season or they were not obtainable. Occasionally we had poached salmon and when I use the term "poach" I do *not* mean, in the words of Madame Prunier, "cooking in a court bouillon—the liquid just gently trembling so that cooking proceeds by a gradual penetration of heat into the fish." I mean it was illegally netted out of season and brought to the kitchen door wrapped in a piece of sacking. It was a far sweeter fish than anything that came from the fish market. There was trout, both lake and river, and lobster that cost the equivalent of 14 cents for a two-pounder. And again in season, we bought oysters by the small barrel.

But the sweetest of all fishes were those that we caught as young people. There were times when more speed than skill was needed to scoop out with our hands the small dark brown trout that found their way into the holes where the peat had been cut. And later, when I could use a rod and line, we caught the small bony perch, the bream, and the lake trout which we cleaned and spitted on willow twigs and cooked on hot stones. One day I brought home a jack pike. My sister, the cook and I were the only members of the family who would eat it. It was stuffed and baked and we promptly got typhoid fever—all three of us. Pike is a fresh-water scavenger and when old, one of the ugliest fish I know. Later in life I met up with that great delicacy, *quenelle de brochet,* made from this unhandsome pike. I have now mastered the art of preparing the quenelle ahead of time and you will find the recipe for it in this chapter.

Summers at the sea, we hooked out crabs from under rock ledges and occasionally found a one-clawed lobster that had taken shelter there to grow another. We netted shrimp in the shallow sandy creeks—shelling them was a chore fit to drive one mad, but well worth it. Occasionally we caught a conger eel that caused enough excitement to last for days. We never made any attempt to eat it but cut it up and used it as bait to catch the fish that we knew how to cook.

When I was at boarding school and taken out for the day, my favorite meal was a mound of filet of sole, crumbed and fried to bright golden with mountains of French fried potatoes—usually followed by meringues the size of canteloupe with vanilla ice cream. The children of the family preferred this meal to any other during those boarding school days. But all I can remember about fish at school were those ghastly fish cakes consisting mostly of mashed potato.

I have selected the following recipes because they are favorites I enjoy teaching in both my adult and young people's classes. Most of them are practical and the messy preparation that a number of people prefer to avoid will be done at your fish market. Fish cookery is a gentle art and overcooked fish is worse than no fish at all. When selecting fish, if the head is intact, look for a bright eye and shiny scales—this will indicate freshness. Smell is another pointer—fish should be sweet-smelling, especially around the gills.

I am sure you will find at least one recipe in this section to suit your occasion.

STUFFED STRIPED BASS

Stuffed striped bass, like stuffed red snapper, is a spectacular dish when presented properly. I allow approximately one pound of uncleaned fish per person. This, after cleaning and boning, will yield about 8 ounces per person. Very little is needed to complete the menu, apart from a salad and steamed potato. This dish is excellent served cold with Sauce Verte, mayonnaise, or if you prefer an extra sharpness, sauce tartare.

1 striped bass (5 to 6 pounds), cleaned
5 eggs
½ teaspoon salt
¼ teaspoon pepper
1 tablespoon finely chopped parsley
½ tablespoon finely chopped chives
¼ teaspoon dried dill
2 tablespoons sweet butter
1 cup chopped shallots or scallions
2 cups dry white wine
salt and pepper to taste
3 egg yolks
½ cup heavy cream

1. Preheat the oven to 425°F.

2. Wash the cleaned bass under running water, drain, and pat dry.

3. Break the eggs into a mixing bowl, beat them, then add the salt, pepper, parsley, chives, and dill.

4. Melt the butter in a heavy skillet. Pour in the egg mixture and stir it over low heat with a fork until it is cooked but not dry.

5. Stuff the bass with the egg mixture and sew up the opening.

6. Oil a baking dish and make a bed of the shallots or scallions. Pour the wine over and place the bass on top. Dust lightly with salt and pepper.

7. Bake in the oven for 25 to 35 minutes, basting frequently with pan juices.

8. Remove bass to a heated serving platter and keep warm. Strain pan juices into a saucepan.

9. Beat the egg yolks, stir in the cream and combine the mixture gradually with the pan juices. Heat, stirring, over low heat until sauce thickens, being careful not to allow it to boil. Serve the sauce separately.

YIELD: 4 TO 6 SERVINGS

SMOKED EEL

Smoked eel revives the memory of an industry that flourished at the turn of the century, not twenty miles from where I was born in Ireland, and reminds me once again that we humans have a basically sound instinct when it comes to diet. A learned cardiologist friend tells me the medicine men have found that eating starches with foods rich in fats reduces the possibility of increasing one's cholesterol level.

The men who worked on the eel weirs—stone structures built across rivers with openings at intervals where nets were placed to catch the eels—worked at night. Their evening meal invariably consisted of boiled eel, just caught, large starchy potatoes, and coarse salt. Eel is rich in fat and instinctively they knew that the starchy potato would help in absorbing it. A fiery local distillation of potatoes, or other root vegetables, was drunk to keep out the cold, and many were the tragedies when one of the fishermen had, as they said, a drop too much and lost his balance on the narrow weir, to be swept downstream and into the eternal night.

When you serve smoked eel, I suggest you refrain from telling your guests what they are eating. I have often found that at the mention of eel people turn from it. But it is a marvelously delicate and rich fish and, like smoked salmon, trout, sturgeon, it requires nothing more than a wedge of lemon and melba toast or buttered brown bread.

It is very, very simple to prepare for serving. Remove the skin, take out the center bone and cut it into slices 2 or 3 inches long.

YIELD: 4 TO 6 SERVINGS

KEGEREE

Also called kedgeree, but I prefer Mrs. Beaton's spelling. This delicious mixture of fish and rice was introduced into England from India and the Far East in the Victorian era when Englishmen and their wives were scattered far and wide over the face of the British Empire. Rice, the staple of the diet in those parts, was livened with the addition of fish and seasonings. The Victorians were great adaptors, and I consider this to be one of their successes. Like most adaptations there are numerous variations. The addition of curry is my favorite, both in the kegeree itself and in the sauce.

In the days of country-house grandeur kegeree invariably found its place on the breakfast sideboard. This was anything but simple in appearance and often included porridge, deviled kidneys, poached eggs, cold York ham, bacon, cold game—pheasant, grouse and partridge in season. One helped one's self. Coffee, tea, and compotes of fresh fruit from the greenhouse—this was a man's meal to be taken seriously before a long day with the guns or hounds.

12 ounces uncooked smoked haddock
1 cup milk
1 cup water
3 cups of your favorite cooked rice, hot
4 tablespoons sweet butter, melted
3 6-minute boiled eggs
3 .or 4 twists of pepper mill
¾ teaspoon curry powder (I prefer imported)
2 tablespoons flour
finely chopped parsley

1. Place the haddock in a saucepan with the milk and water. Bring to a boil, reduce the heat and simmer for 5 minutes. Do not allow it to boil over as it makes a ghastly mess. Set aside to cool.

2. Strain the liquid from the haddock and reserve. Remove the skin and all of the bones, place the haddock in a mixing bowl, and break up into flakes.

3. Mix the cooked rice with 2 tablespoons of the melted butter and add to the haddock, tossing to mix thoroughly.

4. Chop 2 eggs finely. Add to the haddock and rice mixture and season with pepper and ¼ teaspoon of the curry powder. Salt is not necessary because of the salt in the fish. Moisten mixture with 4 table-spoons of the reserved haddock liquid and pack fairly tight in a mold or bowl, level with the top.

5. Combine the 2 tablespoons remaining melted butter and the flour in a saucepan and cook over low heat for 2 or 3 minutes. Gradually whisk in the remaining reserved haddock liquid, stirring constantly. Add the remaining ½ teaspoon curry powder and cook for another 3 minutes. Keep sauce hot.

6. Unmold the kegeree onto a serving platter. Put the remaining egg through a coarse sieve and garnish with this and a ring of parsley. Serve the hot sauce separately.

YIELD : 4 TO 6 SERVINGS

QUENELLES DE BROCHET (PIKE)

This extremely delicate and luxurious dish is considered to be a terrific chore to make. Normally the quenelles are poached and served im-mediately but the method I use is better suited to present-day living. I have found that I can make them ahead of time by partially poaching them and then, just before serving, completing the rising process in the oven. Most people are afraid to tackle quenelles of fish but if you read the recipe through carefully several times and take special care in beating in the right amount of cream, and in shaping the quenelles before poaching, there is very little that can go wrong.

Choux Paste

1 cup water
1 teaspoon salt
¼ cup sweet butter
1 cup sifted flour
2 eggs
2 egg whites

Quenelles

1¼ pounds raw pike
2 tablespoons chopped black truffles
½ teaspoon salt
¼ teaspoon white pepper
¼ teaspoon nutmeg
heavy cream
Sauce Nantua (see page 106)

1. To prepare the Choux Paste which is the basis of the quenelles, bring the water, salt, and butter to a boil. Add the flour all at once, remove the pan from the heat, and stir until the mixture leaves the sides of the pan and forms a ball.

2. Transfer the paste to a large bowl of the electric mixer and allow it to cool slightly. Using the blending attachment of the mixer at medium speed, add the eggs and egg whites one at a time, beating until they are thoroughly blended and the paste is light in texture.

3. Skin and bone the raw pike and put twice through the fine blade of the meat grinder. There should be 2 cups of purée. (An obliging fish market will skin, bone and grind the pike for you).

4. Combine the pike, truffles, salt, pepper, and nutmeg in a bowl and add to the paste. Continue to beat until thoroughly blended. Remove the bowl of quenelle paste to the refrigerator to chill thoroughly.

5.. Before preparing the quenelles for poaching, replace the bowl of quenelle paste on the mixer, at medium speed, and add the heavy cream, one tablespoon at a time. Rarely will more than six table-spoons be required, and usually four will be sufficient. The mixture should be firm enough to hold shape when the quenelles are formed. If too much cream is added the quenelles will fall apart while cooking.

6. Butter the bottom of a large pan and have sufficient boiling, salted water at the ready (about 1 tablespoon salt per quart). With 2 spoons dipped in hot water form egg-shaped quenelles of the chilled pike mixture and lay them in the pan. Pour in enough boiling water to float them. Do it very gently. Cook in barely simmering water for about 6 minutes, turning them once with a slotted spoon. Remove them with the slotted spoon to paper towels to drain.

7. Place the partially cooked quenelles in a well-buttered ovenproof dish, brush with melted butter, cover with foil, and store in the refrigerator until required. They can also be frozen with success. Remember to remove them from the refrigerator one hour (or from the freezer for several hours) to reach room temperature before baking.

8. To finish cooking, heat the oven to 300°F. and bake for 20 minutes. Serve immediately with Sauce Nantua.

YIELD : 6 TO 8 SERVINGS

BAKED STUFFED RED SNAPPER

A whole baked red snapper makes a colorful presentation. I suggest that great care be taken with the garnish, to provide contrasts in color and texture. Very little else is needed with this and I would go no further than a fresh green salad and, for potato lovers, steamed new potatoes lightly sprinkled with finely chopped parsley.

1 red snapper, about 6 pounds
1 cup soft white bread crumbs
1 teaspoon sage
2 teaspoons chopped onion
2 mushrooms, finely chopped
2 tablespoons parsley, finely chopped
1 tablespoon grated orange rind
   salt and pepper to taste

$\frac{1}{4}$ cup dry vermouth (approximately)
butter
$\frac{1}{2}$ cup orange juice
1 cup dry vermouth
chopped parsley
orange slices

1. Preheat oven to 350°F.

2. Wash the cleaned red snapper under running water. Drain and wipe dry. If it hasn't already been done at the fish market, scrape the outside to remove scales.

3. In a mixing bowl combine the bread crumbs (freshly grated or blender), sage, onion, mushrooms, parsley, orange rind, salt and pepper to taste, and enough vermouth to moisten the mixture.

4. Fill the inside of the snapper with the stuffing and sew up the opening. Transfer the snapper to a well-buttered baking dish and dot with small pieces of butter.

5. Bake for 10 minutes. Pour in the orange juice and 1 cup vermouth and bake 15 minutes longer.

6. Increase the oven temperature to 450°F. and continue baking until the snapper is well browned, 7 to 8 minutes. Transfer the fish to a heated serving platter and keep warm.

7. Strain the pan juices into a small saucepan and reduce by half over high heat.

8. Garnish fish with chopped parsley and orange slices. Serve the pan juices separately.

YIELD : 6 TO 8 SERVINGS

POACHED SALMON

Poaching is, in my opinion, one of the easiest and best methods of cooking fish. A whole poached salmon is spectacular for a buffet and will serve a great many people with a minimum of preparation. Garnished with sliced cucumber, parsley, and cherry tomatoes, it makes a beautiful presentation. One need not be confined to a whole fish, however. Thick slices of salmon, turbot, or halibut are equally good prepared this way and should be served with Hollandaise Sauce or Maltaise Sauce, which is Hollandaise flavored with orange. Good accompaniments are small boiled potatoes cooked with a few sprigs of fresh mint, and thinly sliced cucumbers sprinkled with a little sugar and sufficient wine vinegar to cover. A whole striped bass treated in the same way as a whole salmon is a splendid variation.

> 4 quarts water
> 4 tablespoons salt
> 2 cups dry white wine
> 2 stalks celery
> 8 peppercorns
> 1 bay leaf
> 2 carrots, thinly sliced
> 1 medium onion, sliced
> 1 whole fresh salmon (10-12 pounds)
> garnish of cherry tomatoes, parsley, thinly sliced cucumber

1. Use a large fish kettle that will hold the whole salmon on a rack. Prepare the court bouillon by combining sufficient water to cover the salmon, the salt (1 tablespoon per quart of water), wine, celery, peppercorns, bay leaf, carrots, and onion. Simmer the bouillon for 30 minutes.

2. Scrape the salmon with the back of a knife to remove all the scales. Place it on the rack and lower it into the simmering bouillon. Simmer for 35 minutes, being careful not to boil. Turn off the heat and allow the salmon to cool in the bouillon.

3. Lift out the rack and remove the skin and dark flesh close to the backbone of the salmon. Turn it over and repeat the operation.

4. Transfer the cold salmon to a large serving platter and garnish the fish with the cherry tomatoes, parsley, and slices of cucumber.

YIELD : 12 TO 14 SERVINGS

SAUMON EN PAPILLOTE

Fresh salmon as treated in this recipe is absolutely delicious. The sauce takes time but the remainder of the preparation is simple. It is a non-messy method and your guests will be surprised to see their salmon cooked in paper and brought to the table in its own package.

2 medium tomatoes
4 large mushroom caps
1 tablespoon finely chopped shallots
3 tablespoons sweet butter
1 heaping tablespoon flour
⅓ cup dry white wine
1 cup heavy cream
¼ cup finely chopped parsley
6 salmon steaks (8 ounces each)
1 teaspoon salt
¼ teaspoon pepper
3 sheets parchment paper (15 by 18 inches), from butcher
1 egg
1 tablespoon water

1. Preheat oven to 375°F.

2. Plunge the tomatoes into boiling water for 10 seconds and remove the skin. Cut in half, remove the seeds, and dice. Wipe the mushroom caps with a damp cloth and slice.

3. Heat the butter in a saucepan, add the tomatoes and mushrooms and sauté until soft. Add the shallots and cook another 2 minutes. Sprinkle over the flour and cook for an additional 2 minutes. Add the wine and continue cooking for 3 or 4 minutes. Stir in the cream and cook, stirring, until the sauce thickens. Remove from the heat and add the parsley.

4. Season the salmon steaks with salt and pepper.

5. Cut each sheet of parchment paper in half and brush each piece with melted butter. Fold each piece in half, open, and place 2 tablespoons of sauce near the fold. Place a salmon steak on top and cover the steak with 3 tablespoons of sauce. Fold the paper over and pinch the edges to form a half moon shape. Brush the entire package with melted butter.

6. Beat one egg with 1 tablespoon of water and brush the edges of the paper to seal. Repeat the procedure for the remaining steaks.

7. Place the packaged salmon steaks on a greased pan on the top rack of the oven and bake for 15 minutes.

8. Serve in the paper bags. Cut open your own bag first, so that your guests, should they be confused, can follow suit.

YIELD : 6 SERVINGS

SALMON MOUSSE IN ASPIC

Mousses of any kind are frequently off-putting and many people are reluctant to make them. In actual fact, they are very simple to make but they do require time. However, one can always be doing something else while waiting for the aspic to set. This mousse is ideal for a buffet and may be made well in advance—even a day or two. It makes an excellent first course—in a small quantity, as the mousse is very rich. Care must be taken in unmolding. Metal molds conduct heat rapidly and I find that usually a kitchen towel soaked in hot water and then wrung out and wrapped around the mold is sufficient to loosen the mousse. The heavy porcelain molds take more care and have to be dipped several times into hot water. Here, of course, if the mold becomes too hot the mousse will lose its shape and run.

> 1 cup Quick Aspic Jelly (*see page* 111)
> 1 truffle, or a few black olives
> 2 cups fresh poached salmon (approximately 2 pounds raw)
> 3 tablespoons mayonnaise
> 1 tablespoon lemon juice (or to taste)
>   grated rind of 1 lemon
> 2 teaspoons salt
> ¼ teaspoon cayenne
>   scraping of fresh nutmeg
> 1 envelope unflavored gelatin
> ½ cup cold water
> ½ cup heavy cream

1. Place a 1-quart ring mold or fish mold in the refrigerator until it is thoroughly chilled.

2. Prepare Quick Aspic Jelly and cool.

3. Rinse the mold with cold water. Pour in half the aspic and swirl it around, turning the mold until the interior is well coated.

4. Cut the truffle or olives into small, fancy shapes such as stars, dots, etc. and arrange them decoratively inside the mold. Spoon a little aspic over the decoration. Chill the mold in the refrigerator until the aspic is set. Pour the remaining aspic into a flat dish and refrigerate.

5. Flake the salmon and place it in the bowl of the electric mixer. Add the mayonnaise, lemon juice, lemon rind, salt, cayenne, and nutmeg and beat the mixture at high speed until it is thoroughly puréed.

6. Soften the gelatin in the cold water and dissolve it over hot water. Beat the gelatin into the salmon mixture.

7. Whip the cream to soft peaks and fold into the salmon mixture. Place the mousse in the refrigerator to chill.

8. Spoon the mousse into the prepared mold and chill for at least 2 hours, or until it is firm.

9. To unmold, quickly dip the mold into hot water three times. Wipe the base dry and invert the mold on a large glass or silver platter. Chop the remaining aspic into small pieces and use them to garnish the platter.

10. Serve the mousse plain, or with Sauce Verte (*see page* 111) if desired.

YIELD : 6 TO 8 SERVINGS

SOLE MEUNIÈRE

Meunière is a simple way to cook fish and, in actual fact, amounts to no more than shallow frying. Any small fish, slices of larger fish or filets may be prepared in this manner. Variations of Sole Meunière include a garnish of sautéed mushrooms, quartered tomatoes, or whole shrimp. I think this is as far as one need go with this form of cooking. A steamed potato is the appropriate accompaniment.

> 6 medium filets of sole
> 2 tablespoons flour
> 6 tablespoons clarified sweet butter
> 1 to 2 tablespoons lemon juice
>   salt and pepper to taste
> 1 tablespoon finely chopped parsley

1. Dust the filets lightly with flour on both sides.

2. To make 6 tablespoons clarified butter, melt 8 tablespoons butter in a pan, heat, remove from the burner and allow sediment to settle. Pour or spoon off the clear fat. Pour half the clarified butter in a

large skillet and sauté the filets on both sides until golden brown. Remove the filets to a serving dish and keep warm.

3. Add the remaining clarified butter and the lemon juice to the pan juices, season with salt and pepper, and stir until the butter sauce foams. Pour over the filets, sprinkle with parsley, and serve immediately.

YIELD : 6 SERVINGS

FILET OF SOLE IN FOIL

Filet of sole or other fish that filets successfully, baked *en papillote,* is one of my favorite ways of cooking fish. The flavor is retained, the entire preparation is unmessy and the result is unusual. For a more elaborate dinner this can be served as a first course. Or serve it as a luncheon dish, with a good green salad.

> 1 medium-sized filet of sole
> salt and pepper
> butter
> dried dill
> 1 teaspoon lemon juice
> 1 teaspoon dry sherry
> finely chopped parsley

1. Preheat oven to 350°F.

2. Lay the filet of sole on a piece of foil large enough to form an envelope when folded.

3. Season with salt and pepper, dot with small pieces of butter and sprinkle sparingly with dill. Turn the filet over and repeat the process.

4. Fold the foil to form an envelope, leaving an opening. Pour in the lemon juice and sherry. Close the envelope and seal securely. Place in the oven for 15 minutes.

5. Open foil and slide filet and juices onto a hot plate. Sprinkle with parsley and serve immediately.

YIELD : 1 SERVING

SOLE VÉRONIQUE

When preparing Sole Véronique, I often use a dry white vermouth instead of a dry white wine. Vermouth is more satisfactory and is more frequently at hand. Also, an inferior white wine will spoil this delicate dish. Sole prepared in this way is a particularly suitable luncheon dish. Serve it also as a first course for a more formal dinner party.

   1½ cups dry white vermouth or dry white wine
   1½ cups water
   ½ cup clam juice
   ½ teaspoon salt
   ¼ teaspoon white pepper
   6 medium filets of sole
   3 tablespoons sweet butter
   3 tablespoons flour
   2 egg yolks
     salt and pepper to taste
   1 cup white seedless grapes, peeled
     garnish of finely chopped parsley

1. In a flameproof casserole or earthenware dish combine the wine, water, clam juice, salt, and pepper and bring to a boil. Lower the heat, add the filets of sole, and poach them for 5 minutes. Remove the filets to a serving platter and keep warm. Reserve 3 cups of the poaching liquid.

2. Melt the butter in a saucepan, stir in the flour, and cook the roux for about 3 minutes.

3. Remove the pan from the heat and blend in the reserved poaching liquid. Return to moderate heat, stirring to make a smooth paste.

4. Beat the egg yolks in a bowl, stir in a little of the sauce, and then blend yolk mixture into the remaining sauce. Return the sauce to the heat but do not let it boil.

5. Correct the seasoning with salt and pepper and spoon sauce over the filets to cover. Garnish the platter with the grapes and sprinkle with chopped parsley.

YIELD : 6 SERVINGS

SOUFFLÉ OF SOLE AND SHRIMP

Sole and shrimp form a dramatic combination in a soufflé ideally suited to a main course luncheon dish. You can, with proper timing, put it in the oven, have a cocktail, and it will be ready when you bring your guests to the table. You will find there is a certain amount of liquid at the bottom of the soufflé dish. This is unavoidable as it comes from the sole during the cooking time. As an accompaniment, a tossed green salad is sufficient, followed by cheese and perhaps a bowl of fruit.

> 1 pound cooked shrimp
> salt, pepper, nutmeg
> 1 tablespoon lemon juice
> 6 medium filets of sole (1½ whole fish)
> 3 tablespoons sweet butter
> 2½ tablespoons flour
> ⅔ cup warm milk
> ⅓ cup clam juice or shrimp broth
> ¼ cup Swiss cheese, grated
> 4 egg yolks
> 6 egg whites
> 2 tablespoons finely grated Parmesan cheese

1. Preheat oven to 400°F.

2. Place a collar of cooking foil around the top of a 1½-quart soufflé dish.

3. Cut the shrimp into small pieces. Combine them with a light dusting of salt, pepper, and nutmeg, and the lemon juice in a mixing bowl.

4. Cut the filets of sole in half lengthwise and spread about 1 tablespoon of the shrimp mixture on each half, reserving ¼ of the shrimp mixture. Roll the filet halves tightly and place them in the soufflé dish.

5. Melt the butter in a medium saucepan, stir in the flour, and cook the roux for several minutes, stirring to a smooth paste. Stir in the milk gradually. Add the clam juice or broth and the Swiss cheese and cook the mixture over medium heat until it is thick, 2 to 3 minutes. Remove from the fire to cool slightly.

6. Beat the egg yolks until light-colored and stir into the cooled cheese mixture. Stir in remaining shrimp mixture.

7. Beat the egg whites with a pinch of salt until they form stiff peaks. Stir a large spoonful of egg white into the cheese mixture, then gently fold in the remainder.

8. Spoon the soufflé mixture over the stuffed sole filets and sprinkle the Parmesan cheese on top.

9. Bake the soufflé for 40 to 45 minutes, or until golden brown.

10. Serve at once.

YIELD : 6 SERVINGS

BOUILLABAISSE

$\frac{1}{2}$ pound raw shrimp
2 squid (about $\frac{1}{2}$ pound—optional)
2 filets of sole
4 medium tomatoes
1 medium onion
3 tablespoons olive oil
1 bay leaf
1 medium potato, peeled and diced
    pinch saffron
1 small lobster (1$\frac{1}{2}$ pounds)
2 cups water
1 cup shelled raw little neck clams
1 clove garlic crushed with 1 teaspoon salt
    salt and pepper to taste

1. Shell and devein the shrimp. Wash under running water and slice in half lengthwise. Wash the squid and slice into strips about $\frac{1}{4}$ inch by 2 inches. Cut the filets of sole in half lengthwise and cut into 2-inch slices. Peel the tomatoes, remove the seeds, and dice. Peel the onion and cut into thin slices.

2. Heat the oil in a large, deep skillet, add the onion, and sauté for 3 minutes. Add the shrimp, squid, and sole and sauté for 5 minutes. Do not let them brown. Add the tomatoes, bay leaf, potato, and saffron and cook, covered, for 5 minutes longer.

3. Remove the meat from the lobster and cut into large chunks. Add the lobster meat, water, clams, and garlic and simmer, covered, over low heat for 15 minutes. Mix once or twice but do not overdo it as the fish tends to break up.

4. Remove the bay leaf and correct the seasoning with salt and pepper.

5. Serve the Bouillabaisse in soup plates, with crusty French bread and a tossed green salad.

YIELD : 6 SERVINGS

POACHED TROUT

This delicious and simple method of poaching fish may be used also with mackerel, salmon, sole, turbot, haddock, or cod.

6 fresh or frozen trout
½ cup water
½ cup dry white wine
1 bay leaf
1 slice each of onion and carrot
1 tablespoon salt
4 or 5 peppercorns

1. Preheat oven to 350°F.

2. Clean the trout thoroughly, leaving the head and tail intact.

3. Place them in an ovenproof dish and pour in the water and wine. Add the bay leaf, onion, carrot, salt, and pepper.

4. Cook in the oven, covered, for 30 minutes. Cover the dish with foil if it lacks a cover. The eyes will bulge when the fish is done.

5. Carefully remove the fish from the liquid, peel off the skin, and arrange on a heated serving dish.

YIELD: 6 SERVINGS

HOMARD À L'ARMORICAINE

Before attempting this dish, become reconciled to the fact that it is not an economical one, but well worth every penny. Having read the recipe through you may come to the conclusion that it is complicated, and up to a point you may be right. Read it carefully two or three times to become familiar with it and it will present no problems.

3 1½-pound fresh lobsters
5 tablespoons sweet butter
2 tablespoons olive oil
5 tablespoons (2½ ounces) Cognac
2 cups dry white wine
2 large onions, finely chopped
1 clove garlic, finely chopped
½ cup finely chopped parsley
¾ cup tomato purée
1 tablespoon salt
4 or 5 twists of the pepper mill
  dash cayenne
2 egg yolks
⅓ cup heavy cream

1. Cut up the live lobsters; first cut off the claws and crack them to make it easier to get at the meat. Split the lobsters in half lengthwise and separate tail from body. Remove the little bag near the head which usually contains sand and remove the intestines to add later to the sauce, as well as any coral.

2. Heat the butter and olive oil together in a very large frying pan. Add the lobster pieces and sauté until the shells turn red but be careful not to allow the meat to take on color. Transfer the lobster pieces to a large saucepan with a cover.

3. Warm half the Cognac, pour over the lobster shells, and set alight. When cool, remove the meat from the shells and return to the sauce-pan, setting aside the shells.

4. Place all of the lobster shells in another saucepan, pour over the white wine, cover, and simmer for 10 minutes, turning shells once or twice. Strain and reserve wine.

5. Add the onions and garlic to the frying pan in which the lobster was sautéed and cook for 3 minutes. Stir in the parsley and tomato purée, bring to a boil, and pour mixture over the lobster meat. Stir in the remainder of the Cognac, warmed, the salt, pepper, cayenne, and reserved wine. Cover and simmer for 10 minutes.

6. Beat the egg yolks and cream together in a small bowl and stir into the sauce.

7. Reheat before serving, taking great care not to allow the mixture to boil, otherwise the sauce may curdle.

YIELD : 4 SERVINGS

MADRAS SHRIMP

The sauce for Madras Shrimp can also be used for leftover chicken, fish, or beef. Cut up the leftover ingredient and heat it in the sauce the same way you heat the shrimp. Served with rice, this makes a very adequate luncheon or supper dish. The sauce was created to be used with shrimp and with shrimp it is, of course, at its best. The cooking time is barely 8 or 9 minutes. The sauce may be made ahead of time. It can be frozen for future use or stored in the refrigerator, covered, for a maximum of 3 or 4 days.

$\frac{1}{3}$ cup olive oil
2 cups finely chopped onions
1 cup finely chopped green pepper
$\frac{1}{2}$ cup finely chopped celery
1 can (16 ounces) plum tomatoes with basil
1 cup tomato purée
$\frac{1}{4}$ tablespoon cayenne
1 clove garlic, peeled and finely chopped
2 medium bay leaves
    salt and pepper to taste
2 tablespoons imported curry powder
3 pounds cooked shrimp

1. Heat the oil in a flameproof 2-quart casserole.

2. Add the onions, green pepper, and celery and cook until soft, stirring frequently.

3. Add the tomatoes, tomato purée, cayenne, garlic, bay leaves, and salt and pepper to taste. Bring the mixture to a boil and add the curry powder. Lower the heat and simmer the sauce, covered, for 20 minutes. If the sauce seems too thick, thin it with a little strong chicken consommé or water.

4. Add the shrimp to the sauce and simmer for 10 minutes more.

5. Serve with Green Rice (*see p.* 62).

YIELD : 6 TO 8 SERVINGS

GREEN RICE

Prepare your favorite type of rice. For each cup of cooked rice, mix in 1 tablespoon of finely chopped parsley.

SHRIMP NEWBURG

While there are many ways of cooking shrimp in this particular style, my own version of Shrimp Newburg, I find, retains the delicate flavor of shrimp enhanced by the addition of lemon juice. The sauce is enriched with port wine and vermouth. This Newburg can be made ahead of time and successfully reheated just before serving. I serve this either in the center of a ring of rice or in a rather deep serving dish garnished with a border of finely chopped parsley. Further decoration is unnecessary and the contrast of green and pale pink is very effective indeed.

> $2\frac{1}{2}$ pounds raw shrimp
> 6 tablespoons sweet butter
> 4 tablespoons flour
> 2 teaspoons salt
> $\frac{1}{4}$ teaspoon pepper
> $\frac{1}{2}$ cup port wine
> $\frac{1}{2}$ cup dry vermouth
> 1 tablespoon tomato paste
> 1 tablespoon lemon juice
> 2 teaspoons onion juice, freshly pressed
> $\frac{1}{2}$ cup heavy cream

1. Preheat oven to 300°F.

2. Peel and devein the shrimp and rinse under cold running water. Blot them dry with a clean towel.

3. Melt the butter in a heavy skillet, add the shrimp, and sauté them over medium heat until they turn pink, about 6 minutes. Transfer the shrimp to a 2-quart ovenproof dish with a cover.

4. Sprinkle the flour into the pan juices left in the skillet, stirring constantly. Add the salt, pepper, port wine, vermouth, and tomato paste, stirring until the sauce is smooth. Add the lemon juice, onion juice, and cream and continue cooking the mixture for 5 minutes.

5. Correct the seasoning, if necessary, and pour the sauce over the shrimp.

6. Place in the oven, covered, for 10 to 15 minutes, or until heated through.

YIELD : 6 TO 8 SERVINGS

SEA HARVEST

This colorful collection of seafood I like to call Sea Harvest. Serve a small quantity as a first course or serve as a main course for luncheon or supper with rice or noodles. The dish, garnished with an edging of finely chopped parsley, is impressive at table. It may also be served in individual shells or ramekins. Once I made this dish for twenty guests and sent it up to the dining room on a dumb waiter, a very dumb one. There was a crash and we were practically up to our ankles in sea food. I did not have the courage to make it again for some considerable time.

> 4–ounce piece fresh squid
> ½ pound raw shrimp
> ½ pound bay scallops
> 4 tablespoons sweet butter
> 1 tablespoon finely chopped shallots
> ½ cup fish stock or clam juice
> ½ pound mushrooms, quartered
> ½ cup dry vermouth
> 1 teaspoon salt
> ½ teaspoon white pepper
> ½ pound fresh-frozen lobster meat
> ½ cup heavy cream
> 2 teaspoons tomato paste
> 2 tablespoons sweet butter
> 2 tablespoons flour
> 1 teaspoon finely chopped parsley

1. Wash the squid thoroughly and cut into 1-inch pieces. Shell the shrimp, devein, and wash thoroughly. Cut shrimp in half if they are large. Wash the scallops under running water and drain.

2. Melt the 4 tablespoons of butter in a heavy, 2-quart saucepan and sauté the shallots over low heat for 2 minutes. Add the squid and cook until the squid turns white, stirring frequently. Add the shrimp

and cook for another 5 minutes. Add the scallops and cook for another 3 minutes.

3. Stir in the fish stock or clam juice, mushrooms, vermouth, salt, and pepper.

4. Pick over the lobster meat to remove any cartilage. Wash and drain and cut into 1 inch pieces. Add the lobster meat to the saucepan and stir in the cream and tomato paste.

5. Combine the 2 tablespoons of butter and the flour to make a paste and stir into the mixture. Simmer until the sauce has thickened but do not allow it to boil.

6. Serve with Green Rice (*see page* 62), plain rice, or noodles.

YIELD : 6 SERVINGS

SEAFOOD CRÊPES

A supply of crêpes in your refrigerator or freezer is one of the most useful things I know to have on hand. When preparing crêpes for one meal you might just as well make 40 or 50 and pack them for freezing. The fillings one can use for crêpes are legion—cheese, meat, fish, simple jam or preserves, hot syrup, honey, or just melted butter and sugar. But Seafood Crêpes, made with the Sea Harvest, is a perfectly wonderful first course or luncheon dish. Prepare recipe for Sea Harvest (*see page* 63), but for this purpose cut the seafood into smaller pieces and increase the butter and flour to 3 tablespoons each.

1. Prepare Crêpes (see following recipe).

2. Preheat oven to 300°F.

3. Place about 2 tablespoons of the Sea Harvest mixture in the center of each crêpe. Fold the crêpe and place in a shallow, ovenproof serving dish. Repeat until you have filled all the crêpes.

4. Place the dish of crêpes in the oven to heat through.

5. Heat the remaining Sea Harvest sauce, pour over the heated crêpes and serve at once. If you prefer, the filled crêpes may be brushed with melted butter and reheated just before serving. Another variation is to reheat the filled crêpes and serve them covered with hot Sauce Nantua (*see page* 106).

YIELD : 6 TO 8 SERVINGS

CRÊPES

Both the batter and the crêpes should be made well in advance of serving. The crêpe batter is best when allowed to stand for at least 2 hours. The cooked crêpes may be stacked between sheets of wax paper, stored in the refrigerator sealed in foil, or kept at room temperature until ready for filling.

$\frac{3}{4}$ cup flour
$\frac{1}{4}$ teaspoon salt
4 tablespoons milk
1 tablespoon oil
1 whole egg
1 egg yolk
1 cup milk (approximately)
 oil for frying

1. In a mixing bowl combine the flour, salt, and the 4 tablespoons of milk. Add the oil while beating and continue beating while adding the egg and egg yolk. Beat until the batter is smooth and thoroughly blended. Allow the batter to rest for 2 hours or more.

2. Stir in the milk until the batter is the proper consistency, that of heavy cream.

3. To make the crêpes, stir the batter and add more milk if necessary. Heat 1 tablespoon of oil in a 6-inch crêpe pan.

4. Pour off excess oil and place 2 tablespoons of the batter in the center of the hot crêpe pan. Tilt the pan to cover the surface and cook until the batter forms tiny bubbles and begins to leave the outer edge of the pan. Test one to be sure the batter is the correct consistency.

5. To loosen the crêpe, tap the crêpe pan on the outer edge, allow the crêpe to slide half over the rim away from you, and flip the pan to turn the crêpe. This side needs only enough cooking to color.

6. Remove the crêpe to an upturned saucer, brush the crêpe pan with enough oil to coat lightly and repeat the process.

POULTRY

WITH the exceptions of Boned Stuffed Turkey and Capon with Sauce Suprême, the recipes in this chapter are for chicken. These are my favorites, chosen from enough recipes to make another book. There are few parts of the world where chicken is not served at all kinds of tables, rich and poor. Come to think of it, I cannot remember a single country I have visited where I was not offered chicken at least once. It is almost universally liked, not expensive, and lends itself to many dishes which can be prepared in advance, making it an excellent choice for many occasions.

I leave the reader to find elsewhere methods for preparing the traditional roast stuffed goose or turkey. And as for duck, it is too difficult to find a proper one—one with meat and a bit of fat instead of the other way around.

CAPON WITH SAUCE SUPRÊME

Capon is seldom served at home like this and it is so good. The preparation is simple but take care that you do not allow it to overcook. Test it from time to time as poultry varies. It should not be allowed to fall apart or look like a bundle of rags.

    1 capon (about 6½ pounds), dressed, trussed
    2 stalks celery with leaves
  12 peppercorns
    1 leek, trimmed
    4 sprigs parsley
    1 bay leaf

3 sprigs thyme, or 1½ teaspoons dried
1 teaspoon salt
1 onion, peeled
1 carrot, scraped
5 tablespoons sweet butter
4 tablespoons flour
1 cup heavy cream
1 teaspoon lemon juice

1. Place the capon in a large saucepan or kettle and add the celery and peppercorns.

2. Cut the leek down the center almost to the base of the root. Wash the leek thoroughly between the leaves under running water. Add the leek to the kettle along with the parsley, bay leaf, thyme, salt, onion, and carrot. Add water to cover. Bring to a boil, then simmer, partially covered, for about 2 hours. Prick the joint between the thigh and drumstick with a fork. When the juice runs clear, remove the capon and keep warm. Skim off fat from the stock.

3. Reduce the stock over high heat to about one half, strain, and reserve.

4. Melt 4 tablespoons of the butter in a saucepan, and stir in the flour until blended. Add 4 cups of the reserved stock, stirring vigorously with a whisk. Simmer gently till thickened, approximately 30 minutes.

5. Return the capon to the remaining stock in the kettle, to keep it hot and moist.

6. Just before serving, stir the cream into the sauce, thinning, if necessary, with more stock. Add the lemon juice and remaining tablespoon of butter, and correct the seasoning.

7. Cut the capon into serving pieces, place on a warm serving dish, spoon a little of the sauce over each piece, and serve the remaining sauce separately.

YIELD : 6 TO 8 SERVINGS

CHICKEN BREASTS IN CHAMPAGNE SAUCE

This is a *recherché* dinner dish. It may be prepared in the afternoon and the chicken pieces gently reheated in the sauce. A purée of carrots, green peas, or lima beans goes beautifully with it.

4 whole chicken breasts
1 medium onion
2 carrots
2 large mushrooms
4 tablespoons sweet butter
1½ cups Champagne
½ cup heavy cream
3 egg yolks
salt and pepper to taste
finely chopped parsley

1. Remove the skin from the chicken breasts.

2. Peel the onion and chop fine. Wash and scrape the carrots and chop fine. Wipe the mushrooms with a damp cloth and slice.

3. Melt the butter in a heavy saucepan or skillet with a cover. Add the chicken breasts, vegetables, and 1 cup of Champagne. Cook, covered, over medium heat for 20 minutes, turning once or twice.

4. Remove the chicken breasts from the sauce, and when cool enough to handle, carefully cut away the bone. Cut each breast into 4 pieces, place on a heated serving platter, and keep warm.

5. Pour the sauce into the blender, add the remaining Champagne, and blend until smooth, or force the sauce through a fine sieve. Return the sauce to the saucepan or skillet. Beat the cream and egg yolks together, and stir into the sauce. Season to taste with salt and pepper. Heat the sauce gently but do not boil, and pour over the chicken.

6. If you wish to serve this from a casserole, add the chicken to the sauce and reheat. Sprinkle with parsley before serving.

YIELD : 4 SERVINGS

CHICKEN BREASTS WITH GREEN OLIVES

Until recently this was not one of my favorites. However, when my class cooked it not long ago, I changed my mind and it has now found favor with me. I like its appearance and the sharpness of the sauce. It is delicious served with Saffron Rice (*see below*).

3 whole chicken breasts, halved, or 3½-pound roasting
chicken cut into serving pieces
1 cup flour

    2 teaspoons salt
    ¼ teaspoon pepper
    ½ teaspoon paprika
    ½ cup olive oil or salad oil
    1 medium onion, finely chopped
    1 clove garlic, finely chopped
    1½ cups dry white wine
    1 pound fresh mushrooms
    4 medium tomatoes, peeled, quartered
    1 4-ounce bottle small pimiento-stuffed olives
    finely chopped parsley

1. Preheat oven to 350°F.

2. Place the chicken breasts, or pieces, in a paper bag with a mixture of flour, salt, pepper, and paprika. Shake until they are well coated.

3. Heat the oil in a heavy skillet and sauté the onion and garlic until transparent and lightly colored. Remove the onion and garlic and discard.

4. Add the chicken pieces to the skillet and cook until brown on all sides. Dust with half of the remaining seasoned flour in the bag and cook 2 minutes longer.

5. Pour in the white wine and scrape the pan to loosen any bits. Transfer the contents of the skillet to an ovenproof casserole with a cover.

6. Wipe the mushrooms with a damp cloth and slice. Dip the tomatoes into boiling water for 1 minute, remove skins, and cut into quarters. Add the mushrooms, tomatoes, and olives to the casserole and bake covered for 35 minutes, or until the chicken is tender.

7. Just before serving sprinkle the surface with parsley.

YIELD : 6 SERVINGS

Saffron Rice

Add 1 pinch of crushed saffron to each cup of uncooked rice. Cook by your usual method.

POULET NORMANDE

This is one of my favorite ways to cook chicken breasts. My kitchen and dining room are all one and I don't have to desert my guests while I am finishing the preparation. If your kitchen and dining room are far apart don't attempt this for a dinner party unless you are fortunate enough to have reliable help.

        6 whole chicken breasts
           flour
        6 tablespoons sweet butter
           salt and pepper
        ⅓ cup calvados or applejack
        ½ cup white wine or cider
        ½ cup heavy cream
        6 apples, peeled, cored, and sliced
        5 tablespoons sweet butter
        3 tablespoons sugar
           cherry tomatoes
           watercress

1. Remove the skin from the chicken breasts. If they are large, cut each one in half lengthwise. Dredge lightly in flour.

2. Melt the 6 tablespoons of butter in a heavy skillet, add the chicken breasts, and cook 4 to 5 minutes on each side over medium heat, being careful not to brown. Sprinkle lightly with salt and pepper.

3. Heat the calvados or applejack and pour over the chicken. Set alight, and spoon the liquid over until the flame dies down. Add the white wine or cider, continue to cook 5 or 6 minutes longer, and test for doneness. Remove the chicken breasts to a hot serving platter and keep warm.

4. Stir the cream into the pan juices and cook over low heat until the sauce reduces and thickens slightly. Correct the seasoning.

5. Sauté the sliced apples in 4 tablespoons of the butter, sprinkle with 2 tablespoons sugar, and cook until the edges are slightly crisp.

6. Wash and dry the cherry tomatoes. In a separate pan melt the remaining butter, and toss the tomatoes in it over low heat for 1 or 2 minutes. Add 1 tablespoon of sugar. Do not overcook, otherwise they will lose their shape.

7. Arrange the chicken breasts on a serving dish. Spoon a little of the sauce over each breast. Decorate with the apple rings, clusters of cherry tomatoes and sprigs of watercress.

YIELD : 6 SERVINGS

POULET SUPRÊME MEURICE

This is my favorite chicken dinner-party dish. I don't have to worry about being ten minutes late at the table. It will not spoil if allowed to become dry. The color is rich and the flavor rare. Tomato halves filled with a purée of green peas or lima beans and Potatoes Parisienne are perfect accompaniments.

        $\frac{1}{4}$ pound mushrooms
        $\frac{1}{2}$ cup fresh white bread crumbs
        1 teaspoon finely chopped fresh tarragon or $\frac{1}{2}$ teaspoon dried
        3 tablespoons finely chopped parsley
        $\frac{1}{2}$ cup finely chopped cooked ham
        1 tablespoon salt
        5 or 6 twists of pepper mill
        1 cup dry Marsala
        6 tablespoons sweet butter, melted
        6 whole broiler chicken breasts, skinned and boned
           salt and pepper
        1 cup chicken stock
           finely chopped parsley

1. Preheat oven to 350°F.

2. Wipe the mushrooms with a damp cloth and chop fine. In a mixing bowl combine the mushrooms, bread crumbs, tarragon, parsley, ham, salt, and pepper. Moisten with about $\frac{1}{2}$ cup Marsala and 3 table-spoons of the melted butter—sufficient to make the dressing slightly damp.

3. Lay the chicken breasts out flat. Brush with some of the remaining melted butter, and season lightly with salt and pepper. Place 1 table-spoon of dressing in the center of each breast. Fold each side to the center, fold each end to the center, and place folded side down on an oiled roasting pan. The chicken breasts are shaped to resemble a closed fist. Brush each breast with melted butter and bake for 25 minutes, basting frequently with the pan juices.

4. Add the chicken stock and remaining Marsala, and continue baking for another 20 minutes, basting frequently.

5. Remove the breasts to a heated serving platter. Scrape the bits in the roasting pan, and over high heat reduce the liquid until slightly thickened. Pour the sauce over the breasts and sprinkle with finely chopped parsley.

YIELD : 6 SERVINGS

NANCY'S CHICKEN

My great friend and help in work first showed me how to prepare this wonderful casserole. Many of my friends and students have been puzzled by it, and thought the meat was veal, and even gone so far as to label it shrimp. When you make it, double the quantities and freeze what you can't serve. It freezes successfully and is a great standby.

        3 chicken breasts
        4 chicken thighs
        6 small carrots
        3 ribs celery
        ½ pound button mushrooms
          seasoned flour
          butter
          oil
        2 cups chicken stock
        ½ cup dry vermouth
        2 tablespoons finely chopped parsley

1. Preheat oven to 350°F.

2. Skin the chicken breasts and cut into 1-inch pieces. Remove skin from thigh portions, and cut off meat. As nearly as possible, cut the same size as the breast pieces.

3. Wash and scrape the carrots. Slice larger carrots in half lengthwise, and cut on the bias into approximately ¼ inch thick pieces. Wash celery and cut the same as the carrots.

4. Wipe mushrooms with a damp cloth. Cut off stems flush with caps. If small mushrooms are not obtainable, halve or quarter larger ones.

5. Prepare the seasoned flour: 1 cup flour, 1 tablespoon salt, ½ teaspoon freshly ground black pepper.

6. Put the chicken pieces in a strong paper bag with the seasoned flour. Shake until they are thoroughly coated.

7. Heat 1 tablespoon each of butter and oil in a large, heavy skillet. Sauté chicken pieces, a few at a time, until brown, using more oil and butter as needed. It is important that the chicken pieces are sautéed to a rich dark brown, as this determines the color of the finished dish. Transfer the chicken pieces to an ovenproof casserole with a close-fitting lid.

8. Add the chicken stock and bake in the oven for 30 minutes.

9. Add carrots, celery, and vermouth and cook for 15 minutes. Add mushrooms and continue cooking for 15 minutes. If sauce is too thin, cook for 7 to 8 minutes longer without the lid.

10. To serve, correct the seasoning and just before serving, sprinkle the surface with finely chopped parsley. Rice is the perfect accompaniment.

YIELD : 6 SERVINGS

VIRGINIA BAKED CHICKEN

I have served this chicken for luncheons and taken it on picnics with equal success. If small drumsticks are available I cook them in the same way and serve them at cocktail parties when substantial food is required. I suggest that if you have to refrigerate the chicken, take it out at least an hour before serving.

> 1 broiler, cut into 8 serving pieces
> 1 cup sour cream
> $\frac{1}{2}$ cup seasoned bread crumbs
>   melted butter

1. Preheat oven to 375°F.

2. Remove the skin from the chicken pieces and place them in a shallow dish. Cover each piece completely with sour cream.

3. If you prefer to make your own seasoned bread crumbs, for 2 cups of bread crumbs add 1 teaspoon salt, $\frac{1}{4}$ teaspoon pepper, and 1 teaspoon dried thyme. Lift the chicken pieces one by one from the sour cream, roll in bread crumbs, and place on an oiled baking sheet.

4. Dribble melted butter over each piece of chicken and bake for 45 minutes.

YIELD : 4 SERVINGS

CHICKEN 243

I love the versatility of chicken and I find there are few who dislike it. Shortly after I moved to a house numbered 243, I was letting my imagination have full rein, and thinking of other ways to cook and serve the very popular chicken. For want of a better title I named it after the house number. This is what I came up with. I have taught it in my classes and served it to my guests and it is seldom that I find enough left over for the cat.

 2 tablespoons sweet butter
2½–pound broiler, cut into 8 pieces
 3 tablespoons brandy
 ½ ounce dried mushrooms
 1 tablespoon finely chopped onion
 2 cloves garlic, finely chopped
 1 teaspoon meat glaze (Bovril)
 4 teaspoons tomato paste
 3 tablespoons flour
 1 cup chicken stock
 ½ cup dry white wine
   salt and pepper to taste
 1 cup sour cream
 4 tablespoons finely chopped parsley

1. An hour before you prepare the chicken, cover the dried mushrooms with boiling water and set aside.

2. Preheat oven to 350°F.

3. Melt the butter in a skillet and brown the chicken pieces, a few at a time. Add a little more butter, if necessary. Transfer the chicken to an ovenproof casserole with a cover.

4. Add the brandy to the skillet and scrape to loosen all the brown bits.

5. Drain the mushrooms, reserving the liquid, and chop fine. Add the mushrooms, onion, and garlic to the pan juices. Stir in the meat glaze, tomato paste, and flour and mix thoroughly. Gradually add the

mushroom liquid, chicken stock, and white wine. Cook the mixture slowly until thickened, stirring constantly. Season to taste with salt and pepper.

6. Pour this mixture over the chicken in the casserole, cover, and bake for 35 minutes, or until tender. Stir in the sour cream.

7. The chicken may be served in the dish in which it was cooked or on a hot serving platter. Arrange the pieces on the platter and pour the sauce over them. Scatter finely chopped parsley on top.

YIELD: 4 TO 6 SERVINGS

GNOCCHI PARISIENNE

Very few of my pupils or guests have not liked this dish. All the work may be done ahead of time—even the day before you wish to serve it. Remember to take the gnocchi and the sauce out of the refrigerator an hour before cooking time. For a one-course luncheon I serve it in a large flat dish, but for a first course I make individual servings in ovenproof cocottes or ramekins.

Dough

3 tablespoons sweet butter
1 cup water
4 tablespoons grated Parmesan cheese
   salt
   dash cayenne
$\frac{1}{2}$ teaspoon Dijon mustard
1 cup flour
3 large eggs

Chicken Liver Sauce

2 tablespoons sweet butter
6 chicken livers, chopped
1 small clove garlic, crushed with 1 teaspoon salt
3 mushrooms
1 teaspoon tomato paste
1 teaspoon meat glaze (Bovril)
3 tablespoons flour
$1\frac{1}{2}$ cups chicken stock
2 tablespoons red wine
   salt and pepper to taste

$\frac{1}{2}$ cup grated Parmesan cheese
1 tablespoon butter

1. In a saucepan combine the butter, water, cheese, salt, cayenne, and mustard, and bring to a boil. Add the flour all at once, remove from the heat, and stir vigorously until the mixture leaves the sides of the pan. Place the dough in the bowl of the electric mixer to cool.

2. At medium speed, beat in one egg at a time, making sure one has been absorbed before another is added.

3. Have ready a large saucepan of simmering, salted water. With two hot, wet spoons, mold paste into egg shapes and drop into the water. When they rise to the top, they are cooked (about 8 minutes). Cook a few at a time so they don't touch in the water. Drain on absorbent paper. These may be made in advance and stored, covered, in the refrigerator until needed.

4. To prepare the sauce, heat oven to 350°F. Melt the butter in a skillet or heavy saucepan and sauté the chicken livers and garlic for 3 or 4 minutes.

5. Wipe the mushrooms with a damp cloth, slice, and add to the chicken livers. Add the tomato paste and meat glaze.

6. Remove from the fire and blend in the flour. Add the stock, red wine, salt, and pepper. Return to medium heat and cook until the sauce thickens.

7. Arrange the cooked gnocchi in a shallow, well-buttered, heatproof dish. Pour the sauce over, sprinkle with Parmesan cheese, dot with small pieces of butter, and place in the oven for about 20 minutes, or until the cheese is melted and golden brown.

YIELD : 6 TO 8 SERVINGS

BONED STUFFED TURKEY

When I was first introduced to the boned and stuffed turkey, my age was almost a third of what it is today. I was very much impressed. And today I am still impressed. During the intervening years I have learned how to prepare the turkey and enjoy doing so. It takes time and trouble to do well, like any job of work, but the satisfaction at the end is more than compensating.

Make up your mind to go slowly. Try, if you can, to picture where the joints will come and remember to take exceptional care not to allow the knife to pierce the skin where there is only skin connecting the bone. When the boning has been completed, lay out the almost boneless bird flat, pour yourself a celebration drink and contemplate it for a few minutes.

The steps that follow are like those of a jig-saw puzzle—putting it together again takes patience. Take time and keep in mind the shape of a turkey while you are remolding. It's fun!

This is equally good hot or cold and is a most unconventional way to serve the Thanksgiving bird.

1 fresh turkey, 7 to 8 pounds, cleaned, but not trussed
2 teaspoons coarse salt
5 or 6 twists of pepper mill
1 tablespoon lemon juice
4 tablespoons sweet butter
1 small can truffles (7/8 ounces)
3 whole chicken breasts, skinned

Filling

1½ pounds ground lean pork
1 pound ground veal
4 tablespoons finely chopped parsley
4 cups dried chestnuts, soaked, cooked until tender and coarsely chopped
2 cups fresh bread crumbs
1 cup finely chopped celery
½ teaspoon thyme
½ teaspoon pepper
2 tablespoons salt

Stock

carcass of turkey, trimmings, chicken skin
1 medium onion, coarsely chopped
2 stalks celery, chopped
1 carrot, chopped
1 bay leaf
1 tablespoon salt
4 peppercorns
2 quarts water

1. Dry the inside of the turkey and wipe the outside with a damp paper towel. Turn it on its breast, and make an incision along the backbone from neck to tail with a very sharp boning knife. At this point there will not be much meat, so ease the skin off the bone on both sides until the carcass has been exposed. Cut or break off the carcass so that only the breast cage and limbs remain. Taking great care, remove the breast bone, collar bone, wishbone, and thighbones. Always cut and scrape toward the bone so that you do not run the risk of puncturing the skin. So that a realistic shape is presented when the bird is reshaped, leave the wings and drumsticks intact. Reserve the bones you have removed for the stock.

2. In a large saucepan, combine all the ingredients for the stock, bring to a boil, and cook 2 to 3 hours. Strain the stock, and reduce it over high heat to about one half. Boil it an additional 30 minutes.

3. While the stock is cooking, combine in a mixing bowl all the ingredients for the filling.

4. Lay the almost boneless turkey out flat, skin side down. Sprinkle with salt, pepper, and lemon juice. Dot generously with small pieces of butter. Slice the truffles and lay evenly over the flattened turkey.

5. Cut the chicken breasts in half lengthwise—you now have six. Lay three chicken breasts on top of the turkey breast and truffles. Preheat oven to 350°F.

6. Pile the filling on top of the chicken breasts, and shape the bird back into its original form while still on its breast. Lay the remaining 3 chicken breasts on top of the filling where the cut sides come together. Sew up carefully, using small stitches. Push the filling around to give the turkey a natural shape. Fill the neck cavity as well to make a rounded, molded form, and sew up the opening.

7. Brush the entire surface of the bird with melted butter, place on a meat rack in a large roasting pan, breast side up, and place in the oven. After three-quarters of an hour, sprinkle lightly with salt and pepper and add 1 cup of stock to the pan. After another hour of roasting, add 1 cup of stock to the pan juices, baste thoroughly, and dust lightly with flour. Cook another hour and 45 minutes, basting every half hour. (Total roasting time $3\frac{1}{2}$ hours.)

8. If you are serving it hot, remove the bird to a hot serving platter. Skim off any excess fat from the pan juices, and strain into a sauceboat to serve separately. If you are serving the bird cold, allow it

to cool, chill it in the refrigerator for several hours, and brush the bird with strained, chilled pan juices to make a glaze. Carve in medium thin slices starting at the breast and carving straight through the bird. Cut largest slices in half.

YIELD: 20 SERVINGS

MEATS

THE degree of doneness of meats is a matter of personal preference, except with stew and casserole dishes which are usually cooked through. Some like their red meats almost raw; others want them well done to the point of cremation. The French, and many English, prefer lamb pink, and indeed a roast saddle of lamb is considered ill-treated unless the meat is definitely pink. As far as I know, there is no hard-and-fast rule. To each his own. This also applies to the method. For red meats, the choices are: a hot, hot oven to start with, followed by slow cooking at a much reduced temperature; a hot oven all the way through: and a low temperature until the meat is done to your liking. The last method causes less shrinking, but personally I find it does not give the crispness to the outside that I like so much. The chef's meat thermometer is infallible, and is obtainable at most gourmet stores.

Veal and pork should be well done so that there is no trace of blood. By this I do not mean to imply that the meat should be burnt to a cinder.

Most casseroles require meat to be browned in a fat to produce color. An exception, for which I give the recipe, is Braised Beef which is cooked in its own juices and that of the onion, without browning. I thoroughly recommend this method.

With blonde dishes, such as Blanquette de Veau and Irish Stew, the meat is not browned.

With the exception of Lamb Chops Rouennaise, Saltimbocca, and Escalope de Veau, recipes in this chapter leave the host plenty of time to spend with guests. With a little planning, and timing, perfect roasts can be served without spending the entire evening in the kitchen.

I consider roasting of meats one of the great arts in the world of cooking. The English are supposed to excel here, and I believe this to be so. In fact, in the days when the wealthy employed a French chef, as well as an English cook, roasting, whether of meat or game, was always handled by the English cook. So, incidentally, was the making of pies, both fruit and savory.

Cooking on charcoal, whether it be inside or out of doors, I have left to the American reader. In this country it has been brought to a fine art, and on the whole is done much better than I could ever hope to.

CASSEROLE OF BEEF IN MADEIRA

This casserole is ideally suitable as a supper or informal dinner dish, and I often serve it as part of a buffet meal. It is good "fork" food and I like to serve it with well-buttered noodles.

> 2 pounds filet of beef
> ½ cup flour
> 1 teaspoon salt
> 2 to 3 twists of pepper mill
> 3 tablespoons butter
> 1 tablespoon oil
> ¾ cup finely chopped onion
> 1 tablespoon finely chopped shallots
> ½ pound small mushrooms
> 2 cups beef stock
> 2 medium tomatoes
> ⅓ cup Madeira wine
> salt and pepper to taste
> finely chopped parsley

1. Preheat oven to 350°F.

2. Cut the beef in 1½-inch cubes. Dredge the cubes in a mixture of the flour, salt, and pepper.

3. Melt the butter and oil in a large skillet, and sauté the meat over high heat until brown. Transfer the meat to a 2-quart ovenproof casserole with a cover.

4. Add the onions and shallots to the skillet and cook until soft and transparent. Wipe the mushrooms with a damp cloth. Add the contents of the skillet to the beef, pour the beef stock over, and add the mushrooms.

5. Peel and seed the tomatoes and press them through a sieve into the beef mixture. Add the Madeira, season with salt and pepper to taste, cover, and bake in the oven for 45 minutes.

6. Just before serving, sprinkle the surface with finely chopped parsley.

YIELD : 4 TO 6 SERVINGS

FILET OF BEEF IN ASPIC

A spectacular display on the buffet. The pink rounds of beef covered with port-colored aspic are good enough for a picture. It makes portioning so simple, but it is a little heavy on the purse.

  3 cups chicken consommé
  1 cup port wine
  3 tablespoons dry vermouth
  1 tablespoon lemon juice
  2 egg whites
  2 eggshells
  4 tablespoons unflavored gelatin
   whole filet of beef
  6 slices lean bacon
   truffles

1. Preheat oven to 425°F.

2. In a saucepan, combine the consommé, wine, vermouth, and lemon juice. Beat the egg whites until stiff, and stir into the liquid in the saucepan. Crush the egg shells and add. Soften the gelatin in ½ cup cold water and stir into the mixture. Heat slowly, stirring, till boiling point is reached. Remove from the heat and allow to stand for 10 minutes. Strain the liquid aspic through 4 thicknesses of cheese cloth. Allow to cool.

3. Place the filet on a rack in a roasting pan. Lay the slices of bacon lengthwise on top of the filet and roast in the oven for 30 to 35 minutes, or until rare by the meat thermometer. The same cooking time is required no matter what size of filet. Remove the bacon.

4. Cool the filet and slice 1 to 1½ inches thick. If you are the proud possessor of a large silver tray a stunning effect may be achieved. Place the tournedos, or slices of filet, on the tray, or platter, in a pattern which I must leave to you. Chill.

5. Slice some truffles thin, and cut into shapes—diamonds, hearts, clubs, or what you fancy. Dip them in the aspic, and put one piece in the center of each slice of filet. When the aspic has set, spoon or brush more aspic over the slices, and don't be concerned if it runs over the edge of the meat onto the platter. It is best to use the aspic as it begins to set but is still fluid enough to spread. Repeat this operation twice, or until there is a good coating of aspic on the slices. Remove what has run off the slices of beef.

6. Chill the remaining aspic till it is quite firm. Before serving, chop the firm aspic quite fine with a cold knife. It will now look like golden cotton wool. Use it to fill in all the empty spaces between the slices. In my opinion, this is all the garnish needed.

YIELD : 6 TO 8 SERVINGS

BRAISED BEEF

In the introduction to this chapter I mentioned that beef may be braised without browning it first to seal in the juices. Cooked in this manner I find it delicious. Noodles or boiled rice go well with it.

    3 pounds chuck of beef, or flank steak
    2 large onions
    2 cloves garlic
    1 tablespoon coarse salt
      freshly ground pepper
      finely chopped parsley

1. Preheat oven to 325°F.

2. Cut the beef into 1½-inch cubes and place in a heavy casserole with a tight-fitting lid.

3. Peel the onions and chop fine. Crush the garlic with the coarse salt. Add the onions, garlic, and a dusting of freshly ground black pepper. Cover and cook in the oven for 1½ hours.

4. Skim off the fat and test for doneness. If necessary, continue to cook until tender. Correct the seasoning with additional salt and pepper if you think it necessary.

5. Serve sprinkled with finely chopped parsley.

YIELD : 6 SERVINGS

BEEF WELLINGTON (FILET EN CROÛTE)

A fine filet of beef baked in a crust is an impressive sight and a great treat. This particular method is foolproof if you stick rigidly to the timing. The pâté mixture gives a wonderful piquancy to an otherwise flavorless cut of beef. It is often served cold, but the pastry tends to become rather heavy. Puff pastry can be bought by the pound at most reputable bakeries. Serve this with Madeira Sauce if you wish.

> 5–pound filet of beef, center cut, trimmed
> 1 tablespoon dry English mustard
> ½ pound larding pork in strips (from your butcher)
> ½ pound mushrooms
> ¼ pound cooked ham
> 4 chicken livers
> ½ clove garlic
> 1 teaspoon salt
> 2 tablespoons sweet butter
> ⅓ cup dry sherry
> 1 tablespoon tomato purée
> 1 tablespoon meat extract (Bovril)
> 3 pounds puff pastry or double recipe Basic Pastry (*see page* 152)
> 1 egg yolk, beaten
> Madeira Sauce (optional—*see page* 108)

1. Preheat oven to 400°F.

2. Rub the filet all over with the dry mustard. Lay on the strips of larding pork lengthwise and tie with string. Place the larded filet in a roasting pan and bake in the oven for 25 minutes. Strain the pan juices, if any, and reserve.

3. Wipe the mushrooms clean with a damp cloth and chop fine. Chop the ham fine. Trim the chicken livers of any gall and cut into small pieces. Crush the garlic with 1 teaspoon of salt.

4. Melt the butter in a skillet, add the mushrooms, ham, chicken livers, and crushed garlic, and sauté for 3 or 4 minutes. Stir in the sherry,

tomato purée, meat extract, and the reserved pan juices. If you own a blender, blend until smooth.

5. On a floured surface roll out the pastry to a size to completely encase the filet.

6. Remove the strings and larding from the filet and discard. Place the filet in the center of the dough. Cover the filet completely with the mushroom mixture. Fold the dough over the filet and pinch the seam closed, using a little water to seal. Increase the oven to 425°F.

7. Cut out decorative leaves from the remaining dough. Place the filet, seam side down, on a baking sheet. Decorate the top with the leaves and brush all over with beaten egg yolk and water. Bake in the oven for 30 minutes, by which time the pastry should be golden brown.

YIELD : 6 TO 8 SERVINGS

COTTAGE PIE

Cottage pie is marvelous made with freshly ground beef instead of with leftover, as is often recommended. In my opinion, this dish is important enough to be included on a formal buffet. Freshly ground lamb can be used in exactly the same way to make Shepherd's Pie.

> 8 medium potatoes
> 2 tablespoons sweet butter
> 2 medium onions
> 3 pounds ground top round
> salt and pepper to taste
> ½ cup beef stock (M.B.T. or your favorite)

1. Peel the potatoes and cook them in salted water to cover until tender. Drain.

2. Preheat oven to 350°F.

3. Melt the butter in a skillet. Coarsely chop the onions and sauté until soft and golden. Add more butter if they become too dry. Add the ground beef, season with salt and pepper, and cook for 5 minutes, stirring frequently. Pour over the beef stock. Transfer the meat mixture to a shallow, ovenproof casserole.

4. Rice the potatoes, or press them through a coarse sieve, onto the meat mixture to cover evenly. Bake in the oven for 25 minutes. To brown the potato topping, increase the oven temperature to 500°F. during the last few minutes, or put the dish under the broiler.

5. Serve at once.

YIELD : 6 TO 8 SERVINGS

STEAK, KIDNEY, AND OYSTER PIE

A dish as British as John Bull. The addition of oysters causes speculation in the minds of many culinary experts, but, as Sir Winston Churchill so sensibly pointed out, "Why not? We combined the Government Department of Agriculture with Fisheries, so why not do the same in the kitchen?"

Oysters have always been expensive, and not always available, but the pie is equally good without them. The pastry must be good, and in my opinion, short.

> 2 pounds top round steak, sliced thin
> $\frac{3}{4}$ pound beef kidney
> 1 cup flour
> 1 tablespoon salt
> 4 or 5 twists of pepper mill
> 1 quart oysters, or 24 oysters in their liquid
> Basic Pastry (see page 152)
> 1 egg yolk
> 1 tablespoon water

1. Preheat oven to 350°F.

2. Cut the slices of steak into pieces 2 inches by 3 inches. Wash the kidney thoroughly and cut into small pieces.

3. Combine the flour, salt, and pepper in a paper bag. Add the pieces of steak and kidney and shake until thoroughly coated. Remove the pieces of steak and kidney from the flour.

4. Cut the oysters in half, reserving the liquid.

5. Wrap a piece of steak around each half oyster. Place a layer of rolled steak on the bottom of a deep pie dish or 1½-quart casserole, add a layer of kidney pieces, repeat with the rolled steak, and continue

until the dish is full and mounded in the center. Sprinkle with the remaining seasoned flour. Pour in the liquid from the oysters and sufficient water to come halfway up the dish.

6. Prepare the pie crust and roll in one piece ¼ inch thick and slightly larger than the pie dish to be covered. I prefer a thicker crust than is usual in this country. Cover the pie with the crust. Trim the pie crust. Place a long, thin strip of crust around the edge of the dish. Flute the edge and brush with a mixture of the egg yolk beaten with the water. Roll out the remaining pie crust and cut out decorative leaves to arrange in the center. Make a small hole to allow steam to escape. Brush the entire surface with the egg yolk and water and bake in the oven for 1½ hours.

YIELD : 6 SERVINGS

MEAT LOAF DE LUXE

    2 pounds ground beef (top round or sirloin)
    1 pound ground veal
    1 pound ground pork
    1 cup cottage cheese
    1 cup fresh bread crumbs
    1 cup chopped onion
    ½ cup chili sauce
    3 eggs, beaten
    3 tablespoons chopped green pepper
      salt and pepper to taste
    ½ cup Burgundy wine
    1 cup tomato sauce

1. Preheat oven to 400°F. Combine the beef, veal, and pork and mix thoroughly. Add the cottage cheese, bread crumbs, onion, chili sauce, eggs, and green pepper. Season with salt and pepper. Shape into a loaf, and place in a roasting pan.

2. Pour the wine over the meat loaf, and spread on the tomato sauce. Bake in the oven for 30 minutes, basting frequently. Reduce heat to 350°F. and bake until done, about 1 hour, basting frequently.

YIELD : 8 SERVINGS

BRAISED TONGUE

> 1 smoked beef tongue
> 2 carrots
> ½ medium onion
> 3 stalks celery
> 2 tablespoons finely chopped parsley
> 4 tablespoons sweet butter
> 4 tablespoons flour
> 1½ teaspoons tomato paste
>   dash Worcestershire sauce
>   salt and pepper to taste
> 1 cup dry red wine

1. Simmer the tongue in sufficient water to cover for 2 hours. Remove the tongue, and reserve the cooking liquid. When the tongue is cool enough to handle, remove the skin, and place the tongue in an oven-proof casserole or roasting pan.

2. Scrape the carrots and slice. Peel the onion and chop fine. Scrub the celery and slice the same size as the carrots. Spread the vegetables around the tongue.

3. Melt the butter in a saucepan, stir in the flour and 4 cups of the reserved cooking liquid. Add the tomato paste, Worcestershire sauce, salt and pepper to taste. Pour the sauce over the tongue, add the red wine, and bake in the oven for 2 hours.

4. Carve the tongue and put the slices on a hot serving platter. Surround with vegetables and moisten with a little of the reserved cooking liquid. Serve the sauce separately.

YIELD : 6 TO 8 SERVINGS

ESCALOPES DE VEAU

This simple and delicious dish may be prepared in a chafing dish at the table.

> 2 thin slices veal steak (escalopes)
>   salt and pepper
> 2 tablespoons sweet butter

1 teaspoon lemon juice
finely chopped parsley

1. Allow 2 escalopes (4 to 6 ounces) for each serving. Dust them lightly with salt and pepper.

2. Melt 1 tablespoon of the butter in a heavy pan. Sauté the veal slices approximately 4 minutes on each side. They should be lightly browned. Remove to a heated serving platter.

3. Pour off the pan juices and add the remaining butter to the pieces in the pan. Heat until foaming, add lemon juice, and pour over the escalopes. Sprinkle with parsley. Serve immediately.

YIELD: 1 SERVING

FRENCH CANADIAN VEAL

This is an expensive platter but well worth the outlay. Canadian bacon and veal make the friendliest of companions.

3 tablespoons sweet butter
3–pound boned, rolled roast of veal, tied securely
1 tablespoon salt
4 or 5 twists of pepper mill
2 carrots
1 onion
8 fresh tarragon leaves, or 1 teaspoon dried
3 or 4 sprigs parsley
$\frac{3}{4}$ cup chicken stock
12 slices Canadian bacon
$\frac{3}{4}$ cup heavy cream
1 cup Gruyère cheese, grated

1. Preheat oven to 325°F.

2. Melt the butter in a heavy casserole with a cover. Brown the veal on all sides and season with salt and pepper. Scrape the carrots, peel the onion, and chop both. Add carrots, onion, tarragon and parsley. Pour in the chicken stock. Cover, bring to a boil on top of the stove, and transfer to the oven for $1\frac{1}{2}$ hours. Allow to cool.

3. Remove the veal from the casserole. Cut off the strings and cut the roast into approximately $\frac{1}{4}$-inch slices, not quite through.

4. Place the Canadian bacon between the slices, and re-tie the roast into its original shape. Place it back in the casserole and cook over low heat on top of the stove, uncovered, for 25 minutes. If the liquid in the pan cooks dry, add a little hot water.

5. Lift the roast onto a heatproof serving dish, cut away the strings, and keep hot.

6. Pour the sauce from the casserole over the meat. Pour the cream over the roast, sprinkle the grated cheese on top, and place under the broiler or in a 500°F. oven until golden brown.

YIELD : 6 SERVINGS

BONED, STUFFED, AND ROLLED SHOULDER OF VEAL

Stuffing

1 cup fresh bread crumbs

2 or 3 mushrooms

2 tablespoons finely chopped parsley

1 tablespoon fresh rosemary, or $\frac{1}{2}$ tablespoon dried

$\frac{1}{4}$ cup finely chopped onion

2 teaspoons salt

$\frac{1}{4}$ teaspoon black pepper

3 tablespoons melted sweet butter

small shoulder of veal, boned

1 cup chicken, veal, or beef stock

salt and pepper

1. Preheat oven to 375°F.

2. Place the bread crumbs in a mixing bowl. Wipe the mushrooms clean with a damp cloth. Chop the caps and stalks fine and add to the bread crumbs. Add the remaining stuffing ingredients. Mix well.

3. Spread the filling evenly over the fleshy side of the veal and roll loosely. Tie securely with string every three inches along the length. Dust the outside with additional salt and pepper. Place in a roasting pan and bake for $1\frac{1}{2}$ hours, basting frequently with the pan juices.

4. Remove the roast to a heated serving platter and keep warm. Pour all but two tablespoons fat from the pan and scrape the pan to loosen

all bits. Add the stock and cook over high heat until slightly thickened. Correct the seasoning.

5. To serve, cut off the strings and cut the rolled shoulder in 1-inch
slices. Pass the sauce separately.

YIELD : 8 SERVINGS

BLANQUETTE DE VEAU

2 pounds stewing veal
1 large onion, studded with 4 cloves
¼ cup chopped carrots
1 bay leaf
1 sprig thyme
2 sprigs parsley
4 peppercorns
2 teaspoons salt
12 small white onions
5 tablespoons sweet butter
¼ pound mushrooms
¼ cup flour
2 tablespoons lemon juice
2 egg yolks
1 tablespoon finely chopped parsley

1. Cut the veal in 1-inch cubes. Place in a large saucepan and add 1
quart of boiling water. Add the onion, carrots, bay leaf, thyme,
parsley, peppercorns, and salt and cook over low heat for about 1
hour, or until the veal is tender. Test a piece for doneness. Strain
and reserve the veal stock. Keep veal warm.

2. While the veal is cooking, cook the small onions, covered, in 2 tablespoons of the butter until tender—about 10 minutes.

3. Wipe the mushrooms with a damp cloth, slice, and cook in a little
reserved veal stock for about 5 minutes.

4. Melt the remaining 3 tablespoons butter in a saucepan, stir in the
flour to make a paste, add 3 cups of the reserved strained veal stock,
and simmer sauce until thickened.

5. Combine the lemon juice and egg yolks, beat lightly with a little of
the hot sauce, and fold into the thickened sauce. Add the veal.

6. Serve on a hot platter garnished with the mushrooms and onions and sprinkled with parsley.

YIELD : 6 SERVINGS

VEAL MARENGO

Veal Marengo is one of my favorite veal "stews." I once made a vast quantity for a party and had nowhere to keep it overnight except in the garden. A heavy fall of snow completely buried the pot and the hunt for it reminded me of Easter and hidden eggs.

3 tablespoons oil
3–pound boned shoulder of veal, cut into 2-inch cubes
1 medium onion
$\frac{1}{2}$ cup tomato purée
1 tablespoon potato flour
2 cups veal stock or beef stock
1 cup dry white wine
1 clove garlic, crushed with 1 teaspoon salt
2 bay leaves
1 teaspoon dried thyme
  salt and pepper to taste
12 small white onions
$\frac{1}{4}$ pound mushrooms
3 tomatoes
  garnish of black pitted olives and finely chopped parsley

1. Preheat oven to 350°F.

2. Heat the oil in a heavy casserole with a cover. Add the pieces of veal, and cook, uncovered, over medium heat for 4 or 5 minutes.

3. Peel and chop the medium onion, add to the meat, and cook 3 minutes.

4. Stir in the tomato purée and potato flour and mix thoroughly. Gradually pour in the stock and white wine. Add the garlic, bay leaves, thyme, salt and pepper. Cover the casserole, and transfer to the oven for 15 minutes.

5. Peel the small onions. To do this easily, put them in boiling water for 2 minutes first. Cook the onions until tender in enough reserve stock to cover, and add to the casserole.

6. Wipe the mushrooms clean with a damp cloth and slice. Peel the tomatoes and cut into quarters. Add mushrooms and tomatoes to the casserole and cook, covered, for another 30 minutes, or until the veal is tender. Time will depend upon the quality of the veal.

7. Just before serving, add the olives, and sprinkle the surface with parsley.

YIELD : 6 TO 8 SERVINGS

SALTIMBOCCA

Saltimbocca may be cooked in a chafing dish in front of your guests. With a little organizing beforehand it is possible to be with your guests for the entire evening, and not worry about the conversation's flagging while you are cooking. There will be plenty of suggestions and acclamations at your skill, and, I imagine, a lull while the dish is being eaten. This is as it should be.

> 12 thin slices veal
> dried sage
> salt and pepper to taste
> 6 thin slices smoked or boiled ham
> butter
> ½ cup veal or chicken stock
> ½ cup Marsala
> finely chopped parsley

1. Pound the veal slices as thin as possible, and dust lightly with sage, salt, and pepper.

2. Lay the ham slices on top of 6 of the veal slices. Cover with remaining veal slices, and press together firmly.

3. Melt sufficient butter in a large skillet to cover the bottom. Cook the veal until brown on both sides—3 to 4 minutes for each side is usually sufficient for thin, good-quality veal. Add the veal or chicken stock and cook 2 or 3 minutes longer, covered. Transfer the cooked veal to a serving platter and keep warm.

4. Scrape to loosen any bits in the pan, add the Marsala, and cook over high heat for 3 or 4 minutes, or until the liquid has reduced and thickened slightly. Pour over the veal and sprinkle with finely chopped parsley.

YIELD : 6 SERVINGS

VITELLO TONNATO

3- to 4-pound piece of solid veal, cut from leg, tied with string
1 can (7 ounces) tuna in oil
1 small can anchovy filets
2 cups dry white wine
½ sour pickle, coarsely chopped
2 carrots
1 large onion
4 stalks celery
2 cloves garlic
8 peppercorns
4 to 5 sprigs parsley
   mayonnaise
   lemon juice
   cooked rice
2 tablespoons capers
2 yolks of hard-boiled eggs
   finely chopped parsley

1. Place the veal in a large, heavy saucepan with water barely to cover.

2. Drain and flake the tuna. Drain the anchovy filets and chop coarsely. Add both to the saucepan. Add the wine and the pickle. Coarsely chop the carrots, onion, celery, and garlic and tie in a piece of cheesecloth with the peppercorns, and the parsley. Add to the pan, and bring the liquid to a boil. Lower heat to simmer, and cook for 1½ hours. Remove from the fire, and cool the veal in the stock. Remove the veal, cut off strings, and place aside. Remove cheesecloth bag and discard.

3. Place the saucepan of stock over high heat and reduce the liquid by boiling rapidly to about 2 cups of strong stock. Strain the stock through several layers of cheesecloth into a mixing bowl and allow to cool.

4. Stir sufficient mayonnaise into the cooled stock to make a heavy masking sauce. Season to taste with lemon juice.

5. Cut the veal into ¼-inch slices. Make a mound of your favorite cooked rice on a large serving platter and cover the rice with the sliced veal. Pour the sauce over the veal slices. Scatter capers on top.

6. Press the egg yolks through a fine sieve. Sprinkle a border of finely chopped parsley around the edge of the dish, and inside of that a border of sieved egg yolk.

YIELD : 8 TO 10 SERVINGS

ROAST RACK OF LAMB

Ask your butcher to prepare a rack of lamb for roasting, allowing 2 chops for each serving. A full rack of lamb will have 16 chops. Your butcher will remove the chine at the base to allow for easy carving at the table. I suggest no seasoning other than a liberal dusting of salt and pepper.

1. Preheat oven to 400°F. Stand the rack of lamb upright on a rack in a shallow roasting pan and cook 35 minutes to produce the pink, rare lamb prized by many. Roast an additional 10 minutes for well done, but remember that the meat will continue to cook for another 8 minutes or so when removed from the oven.

2. Place the rack of lamb on a heated serving platter.

3. Pour off the fat from the pan juices, add a little boiling water, and scrape the bottom and sides to loosen any brown bits. Bring the pan juices to a boil, reduce slightly, and taste for seasoning. Serve in a separate bowl.

ROAST SADDLE OF LAMB

saddle of lamb (7 to 8 pounds)
1 tablespoon coarse salt
1 small clove garlic cut in half
  freshly ground black pepper
2 tablespoons sweet butter
2 tablespoons olive oil
2 tablespoons dry sherry

1. Preheat oven to 400°F. Trim the side flaps of the saddle, leaving enough to fold under the saddle. If your butcher has not already done so, remove the parchment-like skin. Rub all over with coarse salt and then with garlic. Sprinkle generously with black pepper.

2. Put the lamb on a rack and spread it with the butter and oil. Roast 1 hour, reduce heat to 300°F., and cook 15 minutes longer. Remove the saddle and keep warm.

3. Pour off the fat from the pan juices. Scrape the pan well to loosen any bits. Add 1 cup boiling water or broth and cook until reduced to approximately ¾ cup. Add the sherry, correct the seasoning, and strain.

4. Turn the saddle over, and remove the filet. Carve and place on a warm platter. Turn the saddle right side up, and carve in strips lengthwise. Serve the sauce separately.

YIELD : 6 TO 8 SERVINGS

IRISH STEW

This is one dish on which I consider myself an authority. In my childhood home it was made just this way. It is so simple that it acquires a classic sophistication when served with a flair, and the flavor is unbeatable. To dress it up I sprinkle it generously with finely chopped parsley and serve it in a deep Nankin blue and white dish, usually with only a tossed green salad as accompaniment. There are many variations of this country aristocrat, but in my opinion all others are pretenders.

    4 pounds neck of lamb, cut into chops
    3 large onions
    3 pounds potatoes
      salt and pepper
      finely chopped parsley

1. Preheat oven to 325°F.

2. Trim all the fat from the chops. Peel the onions and slice thin. Peel the potatoes and slice ¼ inch thick.

3. In a large, heavy casserole with a cover, place a layer of sliced onion. Cover the onion with a layer of lamb, and dust lightly with salt and pepper. Add a layer of potatoes. Repeat the layers of onion, lamb, (seasoned with salt and pepper) and potatoes until all used, ending with a layer of potatoes.

4. Pour in sufficient cold water to come three-fourths of the way up the ingredients. Place casserole over high heat on top of the stove and bring to a boil. Cover and transfer to the oven. Bake for 1 hour, or until the potatoes are just tender but not soft. Allow stew to cool and skim off the fat.

5. To serve, reheat in the oven for approximately 30 minutes. Transfer the stew to a serving dish and sprinkle with parsley.

YIELD: 6 TO 8 SERVINGS

LAMB CHOPS ROUENNAISE

> 1 carrot
> 2 small onions
> 2 tablespoons sweet butter
> 1½ tablespoons flour
> 1 cup chicken stock
> 1 bay leaf
> 1 tablespoon olive oil
> 8 rib lamb chops
> 2 tablespoons calvados or applejack
> 3 chicken livers
> 8 slices firm white bread
> finely chopped parsley

1. Wash, scrape, and chop the carrot fine. Peel 1 onion and chop fine. Melt the butter in a saucepan, add the vegetables, and cook for 5 minutes over medium heat. Add the flour and cook until the mixture is brown. Remove from the heat to cool.

2. Stir in the stock, add the bay leaf, bring to a boil, and simmer for 15 minutes. If the sauce is too thick, thin it with a little more chicken stock or hot water. Strain the sauce through a fine sieve and reserve.

3. Heat the oil in a large, heavy skillet and sauté the chops approximately 5 minutes on each side. Remove chops to a heated serving platter and keep warm.

4. Peel the remaining onion, chop fine, add to the pan juices, and cook until golden but not brown. Add the reserved sauce and the calvados.

5. Purée the chicken livers in the blender, or press through a fine sieve, and add to the sauce. Reheat thoroughly.

6. Cut rounds of the bread slices, trimmed of crusts, and fry them in oil until golden brown. Test oil for correct temperature by first frying a small piece of bread.

7. Place a crouton of fried bread under each chop, cover chops with the sauce, and sprinkle with finely chopped parsley.

YIELD : 4 SERVINGS

BONED, STUFFED, AND ROLLED SHOULDER OF LAMB

As with shoulder of veal, the flavor of this lamb is greatly influenced by the stuffing. Shoulders of veal and lamb are avoided by many people. If one is a timid carver this is understandable, but in this case, there is no excuse for avoiding it. The shoulder usually has more flavor, and the meat is of finer quality than the leg. Come to think of it, the leg takes more of the daily wear and tear in both animals. This is another dish that will wait without complaint.

The stuffing ingredients and the preparation are exactly the same as for Boned, Stuffed, and Rolled Shoulder of Veal (*see page 92*).

CURRY

The curries in the United States seem mere ghosts of what I am accustomed to. From that remark do not jump to the conclusion that I am a purchaser, hoarder and blender of the various spices that go to make the curry. I am not, but I have been in the past. And this is the one reason that I am including these recipes. I have decided that I can do without all those additional spice bottles and can produce a very passable curry dish with the use of a reputable brand of curry powder. Risking the wrath of my fellow Americans, I prefer the imported Veraswamis, or Vencatachellum. There are others that bear the Madras curry label that are equally good.

Following are my methods for preparing the dish, using raw beef, veal, lamb, or chicken; a recipe for preparing an excellent curry from leftover meats, fish, or vegetables; and a list of accompaniments which, in addition to rice, go well with curries. The display is colorful and most impressive.

Wine is wasted when served with spiced dishes such as curry, but ice-cold lager or beer is wonderful. Serve curry for Sunday luncheon but first make sure that your guests are curry-minded.

CURRY OF BEEF

For those who like curry, this makes a wonderful weekend luncheon dish served with plain boiled rice, and it goes well on the buffet. Do remember not to serve wine with curry. They simply are not compatible.

> 3 tablespoons clarified sweet butter
> ½ small yellow onion
> 1 clove garlic
> 2 tablespoons imported curry powder
> 1 tablespoon flour
> 1½ pounds top round, cut in 1-inch cubes
> 3 cups beef stock
> ½ cooking apple (greening)
> 6 dried apricots
> 2 tablespoons raisins or currants
>   juice of 1 lime or lemon

1. Preheat oven to 350°F.

2. To make 3 tablespoons clarified butter, melt 4 tablespoons butter in a pan, heat, remove from the burner and allow sediment to settle. Pour off the clear fat.

3. Peel the onion and garlic and chop fine.

4. Pour a little of the clarified butter into a heavy ovenproof casserole with cover, and sauté the onion and garlic until the onion is wilted and transparent. On no account allow it to burn. Remove from the pan and set aside.

5. Mix the curry powder and flour in a paper bag. Add the meat and shake until the pieces are well coated.

6. Pour the remaining clarified butter into the casserole and brown the meat on all sides. Stir in any curry powder and flour left in the bag and cook for 2 minutes longer.

7. Add the onion and garlic, and pour in the beef stock. Peel and chop the apple and add. Chop the apricots into small pieces and add with the raisins or currants. Bring mixture to a boil, and transfer to the oven, covered, for 20 minutes. Reduce the oven temperature to 300°F., and cook for 20 minutes longer. Taste meat for doneness. Correct seasoning and stir in lime or lemon juice before serving.

YIELD : 4 SERVINGS

CURRY OF VEAL

Follow the recipe for Curry of Beef, substituting 1½ pounds veal, cut in 1-inch cubes, and substituting chicken stock for the beef stock.

CURRY OF LAMB

Follow the recipe for Curry of Beef, substituting 1½ pounds of lamb, cut from the leg. Remove as much fat as possible and cut into 1-inch cubes.

CURRY OF CHICKEN

Follow the recipe for Curry of Beef. Cut a small (2½- to 3-pound) broiler in serving pieces, or use boned chicken. Substitute chicken stock for the beef stock.

LEFTOVERS IN CURRY SAUCE

Use chicken stock when you are serving chicken, veal, fish, or vegetables, and beef stock if beef or lamb is the leftover ingredient.

2 tablespoons oil
2 tablespoons chopped onion
2 tablespoons imported curry powder
1 tablespoon flour
1 small clove garlic, crushed
2 dried apricots, chopped fine
2 cups stock (chicken or beef)
2½ cups cubed meat, fish, or vegetables
1 teaspoon fresh lime juice

1. Heat the oil in a heavy saucepan. Add the onion, and cook, stirring, for several minutes, but do not burn. Stir in the curry powder and flour and cook for 2 minutes. Add the garlic and apricots.

2. Remove from the fire and pour in the stock. Return to gentle heat, and whisk until thick.

3. Add the meat, boned and cubed, or fresh vegetables and simmer for 6 or 7 minutes to allow the meat or vegetables to absorb the flavor of the curry.

4. Just before serving, stir in the fresh lime juice.

YIELD : 4 TO 6 SERVINGS

Condiments To Be Served With Curry

Chutney (Major Grey's)
Bombay duck
Papadums
Grated coconut
Fresh orange sections
Raisins (puffed in oil)
Mushrooms vinaigrette
Chopped peanuts
Toasted almonds
Chopped green pepper with onion
Preserved kumquats

Cherry tomatoes
Carrot curls
Sliced radishes
Hard-boiled eggs, chopped
Onion rings, raw or fried
Crumbled bacon
Finely chopped celery
Seedless grapes
Fresh pineapple
Chopped apple

SAUCES

CORRECTLY used, a sauce should complement a dish and in no way cloak or smother it. Sauces present a real problem to the inexperienced cook. They are either too strong, too thick or too thin, or simply not suitable for a particular dish. The proper use of sauces comes from experience and from following in the footsteps of the great chefs until such time as one's own judgment can be trusted.

BÉCHAMEL SAUCE

> 1 cup milk
> 1 slice onion
> 1 chip of bay leaf
> 6 peppercorns
> 1 tablespoon sweet butter
> 1 tablespoon flour
>   salt to taste

1. Combine the milk, onion, bay leaf, and peppercorns in a saucepan and simmer gently 5 to 6 minutes, covered. Strain.

2. Melt the butter in a heavy pan. Add the flour and cook *gently* for 5 minutes, stirring, without allowing the roux to alter color. Add half the strained and, by now, warm milk, mix thoroughly, and add remainder of milk. I use a wire whisk for this operation. Boil for 2 minutes. Season with salt. It is most important to cook the butter and flour as instructed. This will get rid of that starchy taste one associates with atrociously badly prepared "white sauces."

SAUCE NANTUA

    2 tablespoons sweet butter
  1½ tablespoons flour
    1 slice onion
    1 slice carrot
    1 bay leaf
    ½ cup fish stock or clam juice
    2 teaspoons tomato paste
    ½ cup heavy cream
    ½ cup chopped cooked shrimp or lobster meat
      salt and pepper

1. Melt the butter in a saucepan. Add the flour, onion, carrot, and bay leaf, and cook the mixture for 2 to 3 minutes. Remove the pan from the heat and stir in the fish stock or clam juice until the mixture is smooth. Add the tomato paste and cream. Return the sauce to the heat and cook 4 to 5 minutes, stirring constantly.

2. Strain the sauce through a fine sieve and add the shrimp or lobster. Season to taste with salt and pepper.

SCANDIA SAUCE FOR SHRIMP

Whole shrimp, preferably with tails intact, surrounding a bowl of Scandia Sauce, make a perfect appetizer (with drinks before dinner).

    1 tablespoon prepared mustard
    1 teaspoon sugar
  1½ tablespoons wine vinegar (French Dessaux)
    ½ teaspoon salt
      dash white pepper
    4 tablespoons salad oil (or first quality light olive oil)
    1 teaspoon lemon juice
    1 tablespoon finely chopped fresh dill

Combine the ingredients in a bottle. Shake well and allow to stand several hours before serving. This will make enough sauce for 4 to 6 servings.

SAUCE BÉARNAISE

    1 shallot, finely chopped
    6 peppercorns
    1 bay leaf
    1 tablespoon each finely chopped tarragon, parsley, chervil (if available)
    4 tablespoons wine vinegar
    2 egg yolks
    $\frac{1}{2}$ cup (1 stick) sweet butter, softened

1. In a saucepan combine the shallot, peppercorns, bay leaf, tarragon, parsley, and chervil with the vinegar. Reduce over low heat until only 1 tablespoon remains.

2. In another saucepan beat the egg yolks with 1 tablespoon of the butter. Strain vinegar mixture onto the egg yolks. Place the saucepan in hot water.

3. Melt remaining butter till foaming. Pour over the egg yolk mixture in a steady stream. Stir over low heat until the sauce is the consistency of thick cream. Correct the seasoning, but I very much doubt if any correction will be needed.

BROWN SAUCE

    $\frac{1}{3}$ cup finely chopped carrot
    $\frac{1}{3}$ cup finely chopped onion
    $\frac{1}{3}$ cup finely chopped celery
    $\frac{1}{4}$ pound bacon or ham
    6 tablespoons oil, bacon fat, or clarified sweet butter
    4 tablespoons flour
    6 cups beef stock (MBT powder or your favorite)
    2 tablespoons tomato paste
    8 peppercorns
      small bunch parsley
    1 bay leaf
      salt and pepper

1. In a heavy, 2-quart saucepan, cook the vegetables and bacon or ham in the oil for 15 minutes. Stir in the flour and cook, stirring, 8 to 10 minutes, or until the mixture turns brown.

2. Remove from the heat, pour in the stock, and blend with a wire whisk. Stir in the tomato paste and add the peppercorns and herbs. Simmer for 2 hours or longer. Season with salt and pepper. Strain.

YIELD : 1 QUART

MADEIRA SAUCE

Over high heat reduce 2 cups of Brown Sauce (*see page* 107) to 1 cup. Stir in ⅓ cup Madeira wine, and bring to a boil. To serve, reheat but do not boil.

HOLLANDAISE SAUCE

    3 egg yolks
    3 tablespoons warm water
    ½ pound melted sweet butter, warm (not hot)
    ½ tablespoon lemon juice
    salt to taste

1. Combine the egg yolks and water in the top of a double boiler and, over hot water, beat the mixture with a wire whisk until an emulsion is formed. Remove the top part of the double boiler from the heat.

2. Begin to pour in the warm, but not hot, butter very slowly at first, beating constantly. As the mixture begins to thicken, add the butter more quickly.

3. Beat in the lemon juice and season to taste with salt. The amount of lemon juice used is a matter of taste. If you like it more lemony add more, by all means. Personally, I do not like to mask the wonderful flavor of fresh eggs and butter.

4. If the sauce is not to be used immediately it may be kept warm by standing the pan in warm water.

SAUCE MALTAISE

    3 egg yolks
    1 teaspoon lemon juice
    ⅛ teaspoon white pepper

$\frac{1}{4}$ teaspoon salt

4 teaspoons orange juice

$\frac{1}{2}$ cup (1 stick) sweet butter, melted, and hot

1 tablespoon grated orange rind

1. In the container of a blender put the egg yolks, lemon juice, pepper, salt, and 1 teaspoon of the orange juice. Turn the motor on low and gradually add the melted butter in a thin, steady stream. Blend the sauce for about 15 seconds or until it is smooth.

2. Pour it into a warmed sauceboat and fold in the remaining orange juice and the orange rind.

SAUCE MOUSSELINE

3 egg yolks

pinch salt

sprinkling of pepper

$\frac{1}{2}$ cup (1 stick) sweet butter, softened

juice of $\frac{1}{2}$ lemon

2 to 3 tablespoons heavy cream, lightly whipped

1. In a small mixing bowl whisk the egg yolks, seasonings and a small piece of butter until thick. Add lemon juice.

2. Place the bowl over a pan of warm water and whisk until very light. Add remainder of butter in small pieces, one at a time, while whisking.

3. Fold in the whipped cream just before serving. Correct seasoning, if necessary.

MUSTARD SAUCE

2 tablespoons prepared imported French mustard (this is essential)

3 tablespoons boiling water

$\frac{1}{2}$ cup olive oil

$\frac{1}{4}$ teaspoon salt

2 or 3 twists of the pepper mill

1 teaspoon lemon juice

1 tablespoon finely chopped parsley

1. Place the mustard in a mixing bowl and stir in the boiling water. Add the olive oil drop by drop, stirring with a wire whisk, until the oil is completely absorbed.

2. Add the seasonings and lemon juice and stir in the parsley. Adjust the seasoning if necessary.

VINAIGRETTE DRESSING

Vinaigrette dressing is so simple to make that I prefer to prepare it fresh. Fine-quality light olive oil is recommended. I always use an imported French red wine vinegar. The addition of lemon juice is a matter of personal taste. Perhaps the most important ingredient is imported French mustard. I do not recommend making the vinaigrette with anything but prepared mustard imported from France.

> 2 tablespoons red wine vinegar
> 6 tablespoons olive oil
> 1 teaspoon prepared imported French mustard
> 1 teaspoon lemon juice (optional)
> $\frac{1}{2}$ teaspoon sugar
> 1 teaspoon salt
> pepper to taste

Combine all ingredients in a screw-top jar and mix well.

MAYONNAISE

> 3 egg yolks
> $\frac{1}{4}$ teaspoon prepared imported French mustard
> salt and pepper
> 1 cup olive oil
> 1 tablespoon lemon juice or wine vinegar (approximately)

1. Place a mixing bowl on a wet towel to prevent it from careening all over the counter. Put in egg yolks, mustard, and a pinch each of salt and pepper. With a wire whisk or wooden spoon, cream the mixture well.

2. Add about 2 tablespoons of the oil, a drop at a time, while continuing to whisk. As the oil is absorbed, gradually add the remainder. If it becomes too thick, add a little lemon juice or vinegar. Correct the seasoning by adding salt, pepper, and lemon juice or vinegar to taste.

SAUCE VERTE

> 1 bunch watercress
> 2 packed cups parsley
> 2 small bunches fresh tarragon
> 1 pint Mayonnaise (*see page* 110)
> 2 tablespoons lemon juice
>   white pepper (optional)

1. Trim off the stalks of the watercress, using only the fresh leaves. Break off the heads of the parsley and strip the coarse stalks from the tarragon. Wash the greens thoroughly and drain well until free of moisture.

2. Combine the mayonnaise and greens in the blender and mix at full speed. Add the lemon juice and, if desired, the white pepper.

QUICK ASPIC JELLY

> $1\frac{1}{2}$ cups chicken or veal stock
> 1 small onion, thinly sliced
> 1 eggshell crushed
>   white of 1 egg
> 1 envelope (1 tablespoon) unflavored gelatin

1. In a saucepan combine the stock, onion, crushed egg shell, and white of egg, lightly beaten. Simmer for 10 minutes. Cool for 20 minutes.

2. Strain the mixture through 3 or 4 thicknesses of cheesecloth to clarify.

3. Soften the gelatin by sprinkling over $\frac{1}{2}$ cup of the strained stock. Dissolve over very low heat, and add to the clarified stock. Cool before using.

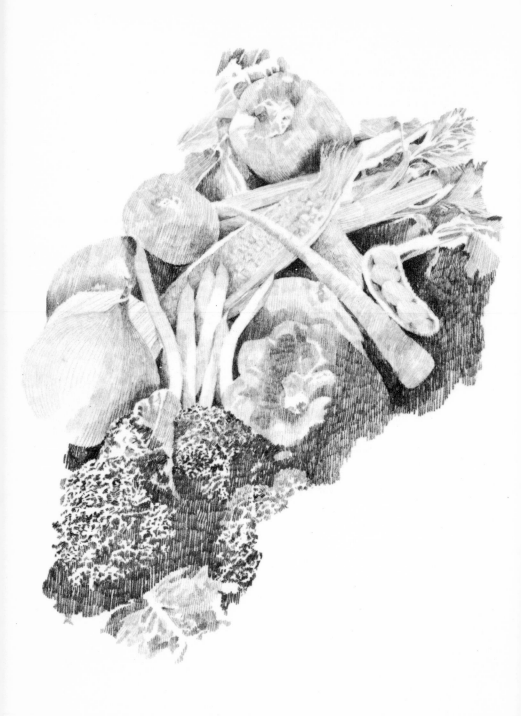

VEGETABLES

MY choices of vegetables for occasions are truly tried favorites. For everyday meals plenty of recipes are available, including those on frozen-vegetable packages. Whenever possible I cook vegetables without water and the cooking time is always the barest. I prefer my vegetables *al dente*. The combinations included here are chosen because they are interesting and colorful.

Today garden-fresh vegetables are hard to find if one lives in a city. Imagination and skill are needed to make the best of what is available.

See also *Appetizers*.

GREEN BEANS

> 2 9-ounce packages frozen whole green beans (or 1½ pounds fresh)
> 3 tablespoons sweet butter
> 1 tablespoon oil
> salt to taste
> 3 or 4 twists of pepper mill

If you use frozen beans, first allow them to thaw. If beans are fresh, wash thoroughly and remove ends. Heat the butter and oil in a heavy pan or skillet and cook the beans over medium heat for 3 or 4 minutes, turning all the time with a large spoon. The beans should be crisp and bright green. Season with salt and pepper.

YIELD : 4 TO 6 SERVINGS

Green Beans with Chestnuts

Slice and cut into matchsticks 1 small can of water chestnuts. During the last 2 minutes of cooking time stir into the beans. The combination is delicious.

BROCCOLI

2 bunches fresh broccoli
2 tablespoons salt

1. Trim the broccoli into individual flower heads, cutting off the coarser stems.

2. Bring two quarts of water to a boil in a heavy saucepan. Add the salt and broccoli, and cook at a fast boil for 3 or 4 minutes. If you can pack the broccoli into the saucepan stem down this is an advantage because the stalks will be cooked, and the green heads will not fall apart.

3. Serve with either Hollandaise Sauce (*page* 108), or Mustard Sauce (*page* 109). I like to serve broccoli in this way as a separate course.

YIELD : 4 TO 6 SERVINGS

BRUSSELS SPROUTS WITH CHESTNUTS

2 pounds Brussels sprouts
2 tablespoons sweet butter
1 cup cooked chestnuts, coarsely chopped
salt and pepper to season

1. Trim off the stalks and outside leaves from the Brussels sprouts. If the sprouts are large, cut a cross into the base of the stalk. Place the sprouts in fiercely boiling water and cook for 5 to 6 minutes. In my opinion, Brussels sprouts should be very crisp.

2. Drain thoroughly. Return to the pan with the butter and chestnuts. Toss and season to taste with salt and freshly ground black pepper.

YIELD : 4 TO 6 SERVINGS

CARROTS VICHY

      6 to 8 medium carrots
      3 tablespoons sweet butter
      1 tablespoon water
      1 teaspoon salt
      3 or 4 twists pepper mill
      1 tablespoon sugar
        finely chopped parsley

1. Wash, scrape, and slice the carrots paper thin.

2. Melt the butter with the water in a heavy saucepan with a close-fitting lid. Add salt, pepper, and sugar. Stir in the sliced carrots, coating each one. Cook covered, over a low flame, for 4 or 5 minutes. Test for doneness. They should still be crisp. Cook for 2 minutes longer with the lid off. The moisture will have evaporated, and the carrots will have acquired a bright glaze.

3. Correct the seasoning and serve sprinkled with finely chopped parsley. If the lid is not close fitting it may be necessary to add additional water to prevent the carrots from burning.

YIELD : 4 TO 6 SERVINGS

CARROTS, CELERY, AND GREEN BEANS

      2 carrots
      2 ribs celery
      1 9-ounce package frozen whole green beans
      2 tablespoons sweet butter
      1 tablespoon oil
        salt and pepper to season
      $\frac{1}{2}$ teaspoon sugar

1. Wash and scrape the carrots and slice them on the bias about $\frac{1}{4}$ inch thick. Wash the celery and slice on the bias the same thickness. Thaw the green beans.

2. Heat the butter and oil in a large, heavy skillet or a large deep saucepan. Add the carrots and cook 3 or 4 minutes, stirring. Add the celery and cook another 3 or 4 minutes. Stir in the green beans and continue cooking for 5 minutes. Season lightly with salt, pepper, and sugar.

YIELD: 4 TO 6 SERVINGS

CAULIFLOWER

1 medium cauliflower, or 2 small ones
2 tablespoons salt

1. Break up the cauliflower into flower heads; cut off the coarser stems. Soak in cold water and drain.

2. Bring to a boil 2 quarts of water with the salt. Add the cauliflower. If you have a piece of toast left over from breakfast, place it on top. This should absorb any unpleasant odor. Cook, uncovered, for 5 or 6 minutes and drain.

3. If you wish to serve cauliflower *au gratin,* arrange it on the bottom of an ovenproof dish and sprinkle liberally with bread crumbs that have been tossed in butter. Dot with additional butter. Heat for 15 to 20 minutes in a 300°F. oven and serve.

4. If you wish to serve the cauliflower with Mustard Sauce (*see page* 109) arrange it on the bottom of a serving dish, trickle a little melted butter over it, and sprinkle with finely chopped parsley. Serve hot, passing the Mustard Sauce separately.

YIELD: 4 TO 6 SERVINGS

JERUSALEM ARTICHOKES

The Jerusalem artichoke has no relation to the green artichoke, and is, in fact, the most tortured, nobby tuber known to man. Its preparation will put a severe strain on your sanity, but the risk is well worth while.

3 pounds Jerusalem artichokes
2 tablespoons salt
melted butter
1 tablespoon lemon juice (optional)
salt and pepper to season

1. Wash and peel the Jerusalem artichokes. As you peel them, place them in a bowl of acidulated water (1 tablespoon vinegar to 1 quart water) until you are ready to cook them. This prevents them from turning black.

2. Add the salt to 2 quarts of water and bring to a rolling boil. Throw in the artichokes and cook for 5 to 6 minutes, depending upon their size and age. They should be firm and holding their shape. Drain and serve hot tossed in a little melted butter. If you wish, stir in the lemon juice. Correct the seasoning with salt and pepper.

YIELD : 4 TO 6 SERVINGS

DUCHESS POTATOES

Potatoes prepared this way are usually used as a garnish.

    1½ pounds potatoes
    1 tablespoon butter
    2 egg yolks
    ¼ cup hot milk, approximately
      salt and pepper

1. Boil the potatoes in their jackets in salted water. Peel and rub through a sieve.

2. Mix the sieved potatoes with the butter in a heavy pan. Beat in one egg yolk and enough hot milk to make a firm purée. Season with salt and pepper.

3. Fit a pastry bag with a large rose tube or star tube. Pipe shapes to your liking onto a greased baking sheet. Brush with remaining egg yolk mixed with a tablespoon of cold water. Brown under the broiler, or in a 450°F. oven.

LYONNAISE POTATOES

    2 pounds potatoes
    2 tablespoons oil
    2 tablespoons sweet butter
      salt and pepper
    1 medium onion, sliced thin
    1 tablespoon finely chopped parsley

1. Wash the potatoes and boil in their jackets until tender. Drain and when cool enough to handle, peel and slice about $\frac{1}{4}$ inch thick.

2. Heat the oil in a heavy frying pan and add the butter. Slide in all the potatoes, dust lightly with salt and pepper, and sauté, turning them occasionally, until they are brown and crisp. Remove the potatoes to a heated serving dish.

3. Sauté the onion in the same pan, adding a little butter and oil if necessary. Cook until golden brown but on no account allow the onion to burn. Mix with the sautéed potatoes. Correct the seasoning.

4. Serve hot, sprinkled with parsley.

YIELD : 4 TO 6 SERVINGS

POTATOES PARISIENNE

6 large "old" potatoes
4 tablespoons sweet butter
2 tablespoons oil
salt and pepper to taste
finely chopped parsley

1. Peel and wash the potatoes. With a melon baller, scoop out potato balls and place them immediately in a bowl of iced water until ready to cook.

2. Heat the butter and oil in a heavy skillet. Drain and dry the potato balls. Sauté them in the hot oil and butter, turning constantly until they are crisp and brown on the outside, about 7 or 8 minutes. By this time they should be cooked on the inside but, to make sure, test one.

3. Season with salt and pepper and serve hot, sprinkled with parsley.

YIELD : 4 TO 6 SERVINGS

POTATO PURÉE

2 pounds potatoes
1 tablespoon sweet butter
$\frac{1}{2}$ pint hot milk
salt and pepper to season

1. Peel the potatoes and boil them in salted water until tender. Drain.

2. Force the potatoes through a sieve or moule sieve. Beat in the butter and gradually add the hot milk. Whip until light and season with salt and pepper. I find a wire whisk produces the best result.

YIELD : 4 TO 6 SERVINGS

SNOW PEAS

Snow peas cooked in this way should be emerald green and very crisp.

> 1 pound fresh or frozen snow peas
> 2 tablespoons oil
> salt and pepper to season
> 1 teaspoon lemon juice

1. Wash the peas and, with a sharp knife, remove the stalk ends and the tips of the pods. If the peas are very young and tender there should be no need to remove the fiber around the outside edge. Heat the oil in a heavy pan. Throw in the snow peas all at once and cook over high heat for 3 to 4 minutes, turning and stirring all the time so that each pod is cooked.

2. Season with salt and pepper, and sprinkle with lemon juice. Toss, and serve hot.

YIELD : 4 TO 6 SERVINGS

SPINACH EN BRANCHE

> 2 pounds fresh spinach
> 1 teaspoon salt
> few scrapings of nutmeg
> 2 tablespoons melted sweet butter
> lemon juice to taste

1. Remove the coarse stems from the spinach leaves, and wash leaves thoroughly in 2 or 3 changes of cold water. Drain but do not dry.

2. Heat a heavy pan, throw in the spinach, and sprinkle with salt and nutmeg. Turn up the heat, toss and stir for 2 or 3 minutes, by which

time the spinach should be wilted and be cooked. No additional water is necessary, as sufficient water will adhere to the leaves.

3. Drain, and press out excess moisture. Serve with melted butter, lemon juice, or a sauce of your choice if you prefer it.

YIELD : 4 TO 6 SERVINGS

CREAMED SPINACH

2 pounds fresh spinach
1 teaspoon salt
few scrapings nutmeg
3 or 4 tablespoons heavy cream
salt and pepper to taste

1. Remove the coarse stems from the spinach leaves and wash leaves thoroughly in 2 or 3 changes of cold water. This is necessary as spinach is usually liberally coated with sand. Drain but do not dry.

2. Heat a large, heavy pan, throw in the spinach, and sprinkle with salt and nutmeg. Turn up the heat and toss and stir for 2 or 3 minutes, by which time the spinach should be cooked. No additional water is necessary, as sufficient will adhere to the leaves.

3. Drain, and press out excess moisture. Place the spinach in the blender with the cream and blend until smooth.

4. Reheat the spinach in a saucepan and correct the seasoning. You may find that a little more nutmeg is an improvement.

YIELD : 4 TO 6 SERVINGS

SUMMER SQUASH AND PLUM TOMATOES

3 small summer squash
4 or 5 plum tomatoes
2 tablespoons sweet butter
1 tablespoon oil
salt and pepper to season
finely chopped parsley

1. Wash the squash, cut off both ends, and dice. Do not peel. Plunge the tomatoes into boiling water for 1 minute and remove the skins. Cut each into about 8 pieces.

2. Heat the butter and oil in a heavy skillet, add the squash, and cook 4 to 5 minutes, turning constantly. Add the tomatoes and cook 1 minute longer. Season with salt and pepper. Serve hot, sprinkled with parsley.

YIELD : 4 TO 6 SERVINGS

TOMATOES PROVENCALE

> $\frac{3}{4}$ pound potatoes, approximately
> 1 pound tomatoes, approximately
> 3 large onions
> 4 tablespoons oil
> salt and pepper
> few scrapings nutmeg
> $\frac{1}{4}$ teaspoon thyme
> $\frac{1}{4}$ teaspoon tarragon
> $\frac{1}{2}$ cup dried bread crumbs
> melted butter

1. Preheat oven to 325°F. Boil the potatoes in their jackets, peel, and slice. Scald, peel, and slice the tomatoes. Peel the onions and slice in thin rings.

2. Heat the oil in a heavy skillet and sauté the onions until brown, being careful not to burn them.

3. Put a tablespoon of the oil from the skillet into an ovenproof dish. Using half the tomatoes, cover the bottom of the dish. Scatter $\frac{1}{3}$ of the onions on top of the tomatoes. Dust lightly with salt, pepper, nutmeg, and a little of the thyme and tarragon. Add the potatoes in a layer. Season with salt, pepper, nutmeg, and herbs, and add another $\frac{1}{3}$ of the onions. Add the remaining tomatoes, and spoon the remaining onions and oil from the skillet on top. Toss the bread crumbs in melted butter and sprinkle on top.

4. Bake in the oven for 25 to 30 minutes.

YIELD : 6 SERVINGS

TOMATOES STUFFED WITH POTATO PURÉE

3 medium tomatoes
Potato Purée (*see page* 118)
1 tablespoon finely chopped parsley

1. Preheat oven to 350°F.

2. Halve the tomatoes crosswise and, with a spoon, scoop out the centers, being careful not to break the skins.

3. With a pastry bag fitted with a large star tube fill the tomato halves, mounding the purée.

4. Bake for approximately 20 minutes. Sprinkle with parsley before serving.

YIELD : 6 SERVINGS

ZUCCHINI, CELERY, AND MUSHROOMS

3 medium zucchini
2 ribs celery
4 firm mushrooms
2 tablespoons sweet butter
1 tablespoon oil
salt and pepper to season
½ teaspoon sugar

1. Wash the zucchini and slice in rounds approximately ⅛ inch thick. Do not peel. Wash the celery and slice on the bias the same thickness. Cut off the stems of the mushrooms flush with the caps; wipe the caps with a damp cloth and slice thin.

2. Heat the butter and oil in a heavy skillet; add the sliced celery and cook for 2 minutes. Add the zucchini and cook for 4 to 5 minutes, turning and stirring. While the vegetables are still crisp, add the mushrooms and cook 2 minutes longer. Season with salt, pepper, and sugar.

YIELD : 4 TO 6 SERVINGS

DESSERTS

THE *pièce de résistance* of almost any meal is the dessert—it plays the part of a precious jewel in an important ensemble, and more often than not is responsible for the success or failure of the meal. It is, as it were, the parting shot—the last course of the meal and the one by which it is remembered.

It is therefore important that much thought be given to the choice of the dessert. It need not be a production—a beautifully arranged bowl of carefully chosen seasonal fruit is often a perfect finale. What is important is that the dessert complement what has gone before: a rich trifle might follow a light entrée but would be disastrous after a heavy casserole. A fine choice to follow a rich main course is a cold soufflé, light in texture and deliciously refreshing. Such a choice is also good because it can be prepared ahead of time.

Desserts may be calorie laden but it is a pity to do without them if you love them. Instead, enjoy them, and cut out something the next day— and the day after that, if necessary. As the London cockney says, "A little bit of what you fancy does you good." Remember, too, that a dish may be made with liberal lashings of cream and sugar, but divided among a number of guests it's not really that much per person. Explain this to your guests if they suspect you of sabotage.

COMPOTE OF FRUITS

This delightful compote may be made days ahead of time except for the strawberries, which must be added just before serving, or they will become mushy and lose their wonderful color.

1 cup sugar
juice of 1 large lemon
2 pears, peeled and sliced
⅓ cup seedless green grapes
⅓ cup red grapes, seeds removed
2 bananas, sliced
2 apples, peeled, cored, and sliced
3 seedless oranges, peeled and separated into wedges
4 dried figs, sliced
⅓ cup water
½ cup apricot jam
⅓ cup kirsch or cognac
1 cup fresh strawberries, hulled

1. Pour ⅔ cup of the sugar into a large crock. Stir in the lemon juice and add all the fruit except the strawberries.

2. In a saucepan combine the remaining ⅓ cup sugar, the water, and the apricot jam. Cook the mixture, stirring, until it is thick. Force it through a sieve, and stir in the kirsch or cognac.

3. Pour the sauce over the fruit mixture and stir it well. Store the compote in the refrigerator.

4. Before serving, stir in the fresh strawberries.

YIELD : 10 SERVINGS

FRIAR'S OMELET

This old English recipe, redolent of apples and cinnamon, is hearty fare and wonderful on a cold winter's day.

1 tablespoon butter
½ cup white bread crumbs
2 pounds tart cooking apples
⅔ cup water
¼ cup granulated sugar, or more to taste
2 eggs
1 cup brown sugar
½ teaspoon cinnamon
¼ teaspoon ground cloves
whipped cream

1. Preheat the oven to 350°F. Spread the butter over the sides and bottom of a 2-quart soufflé dish or pie plate. Sprinkle it with bread crumbs, reserving some for the top of the omelet.

2. Peel, core, and slice the apples and cook them with the water until they are soft. Add the granulated sugar and cook 2 minutes longer. The yield should be approximately 2½ cups purée. Beat the mixture with a whisk until it is smooth.

3. Beat the eggs and mix in the brown sugar, cinnamon, cloves, and apple purée. Pour the mixture into the prepared dish and bake it for 45 minutes.

4. To serve, sprinkle with the reserved bread crumbs, and serve it while still hot, topped with whipped cream.

YIELD : 4 TO 6 SERVINGS

ORANGE CARAMEL

A lovely, fresh-tasting dessert and very simple to make. The oranges and caramel may be prepared ahead of time, but not combined until serving time.

12 oranges
40 lumps of sugar
¼ cup cold water
2 cups heavy cream, whipped
4 tablespoons chopped almonds

1. Peel the oranges, cut them into bite-sized pieces, and put them in a large serving bowl.

2. In a saucepan combine the sugar and water. Cook, stirring constantly, until the syrup is dark brown and caramelized.

3. Spread the caramel out on a lightly oiled, rimless cookie sheet and let it cool completely.

4. Break the hard caramel into small pieces and sprinkle them over the oranges. Cover the mixture with the whipped cream and sprinkle on the chopped almonds.

YIELD : 12 TO 14 SERVINGS

POACHED PEAR COMPOTE

A compote of fresh fruit is a wonderful standby. There are many times when I have it at breakfast. Any fresh fruit may be prepared according to this recipe, and apples are an especially good substitute for the pears. The syrup may be varied by substituting 2 cups apricot nectar for 2 cups of the water, or the fruit may be poached in a mixture of red wine and lemon juice and sugar to taste instead of in the syrup.

>   2 cups sugar
>   4 cups water
>   1 teaspoon vanilla
>   1 lemon, sliced
>   6 pears, under-ripe

1. Make a syrup. In a saucepan combine the sugar, water, vanilla, and lemon slices. Bring the syrup to a boil and boil it for 3 minutes. If you prefer, as I do, a thicker syrup, boil it until you have the consistency you like.

2. Peel and core the pears and cut a slice from the bottoms so they will stand upright. Put the pears in the syrup and simmer them until they are tender but not mushy—the cooking time will depend on the ripeness of the fruit. Test for doneness with a knife, fork, or toothpick.

3. Remove the pears to dessert plates, spoon a little of the syrup over each one, and let them cool before serving.

YIELD : 6 SERVINGS

POIRES NOIRES

>   1 cup sugar
>   4 cups water
>   juice of 1 lemon
>   2 sticks cinnamon
>   4 whole cloves
>   6 firm pears (Anjou or Comice preferably), with stems intact
>   4 squares (4 ounces) unsweetened chocolate
>   2 squares (2 ounces) semi-sweet chocolate
>   ½ cup (1 stick) sweet butter, softened
>   crystallised mint (optional)

1. Dissolve the sugar in the water. Add the lemon juice and spices and simmer in a pan with a tight-fitting lid for 10 to 15 minutes.

2. Peel the pears carefully and cut a slice off the bottom of each so that they will remain upright. Leave stems intact.

3. Poach them in the gently boiling syrup until tender, 30 to 40 minutes. Time will depend on the ripeness of the pears. Test with a toothpick if you are in doubt.

4. Allow pears to cool in the syrup and then chill thoroughly, preferably overnight.

5. Melt all the chocolate in a bowl over warm water. Add the butter and stir until butter is melted and mixture is smooth.

6. Remove the chilled pears from the syrup and dry gently. Dip pears in the melted chocolate to coat evenly. (Use a spoon, if necessary.)

7. Lift pears to drain off excess chocolate. Arrange them on a serving dish—preferably a white one.

8. Decorate the top of each pear with a sprig of crystallised mint or any other suitable greenery you may happen to have. The pears will keep satisfactorily for up to 36 hours. After that they are inclined to weep.

YIELD : 6 SERVINGS

RASPBERRY FOOL

"Fools" are English country food, and the most English of all is made from gooseberries. Use the same quantity of gooseberries as raspberries and you won't regret it.

> 2 10-ounce packages frozen raspberries
> 1 cup heavy cream

1. Thaw the raspberries and drain them. Reserve the juice.

2. Press the fruit through a fine sieve, taking care not to allow any of the seeds to get through. The result should be 1 cup of heavy purée. If it is too thick, add a little of the juice. Sugar may be added if desired.

3. Whip the cream until it is thick and holds very definite peaks.

4. Fold in the fruit purée and spoon into small wine glasses, or serve in a glass bowl. Chill before serving.

YIELD : 6 SERVINGS

SABAYON FRAPPÉ

Sabayon Frappé may be frozen as you would ice cream. Take it out of the freezer and put it in the refrigerator half an hour before serving. It regains its creaminess.

> 3 egg yolks
> 1 whole egg
> ½ cup sugar
> 4 to 8 tablespoons rum or Madeira
> ½ cup heavy cream
> 1 tablespoon grated orange rind or lemon rind

1. Whisk the egg yolks, egg, sugar, and rum or Madeira in a large bowl till all the ingredients are blended together.

2. Place the bowl over a pan of simmering water and whisk till frothy and stiff. This can take up to 10 minutes. Remove from the pan, place the bowl in ice-cold water and whisk the mixture till cold.

3. Whip the cream until stiff, and fold into the mixture. Spoon into a serving dish, or individual dishes, and leave in the freezer for at least an hour before serving.

YIELD : 4 SERVINGS

FROZEN BOMBE

> 1 pint pistachio ice cream
> 1 pint strawberry ice cream
> ½ pint vanilla ice cream
> 1 cup heavy cream
> ¼ cup glacé cherries, chopped
> ½ cup crushed Italian macaroons
> 2 tablespoons Maraschino or Cointreau liqueur

1. If you do not have a melon mold, a 1-quart metal mixing bowl will serve the purpose. Chill the mold in the freezer. Remove ice creams from freezer and put in the refrigerator.

2. Line the chilled mold with 1 pint of pistachio ice cream, using fingers to shape it to the mold. Return to the freezer for 10 minutes.

3. Smooth a layer of strawberry ice cream over the pistachio and freeze again.

4. Use the vanilla ice cream to make a final layer and return the mold to the freezer. There should be a hollow in the center.

5. Whip the cream to form soft peaks only. Fold in the cherries, macaroon crumbs, and liqueur. Freeze the cream mixture until it is heavy, at least 15 minutes.

6. Spoon the cream into the center of the bombe. Cover and freeze for at least 6 hours. If you are using a mixing bowl, cover with plastic wrap and seal the top with foil.

7. Unmold with care. Dipping once into hot water should do it. If you use a porcelain bowl more time is required. It is not as good a conductor of heat as metal.

YIELD : 6 TO 8 SERVINGS

TOASTED ALMOND PARFAIT

This lovely dessert may be kept for a month in the freezer, securely sealed.

> 6–ounce package of almonds, unskinned
> $\frac{3}{4}$ cup maple syrup, or more
> 2 pints vanilla ice cream, softened
> whipped cream

1. Preheat the oven to 400°F.

2. Spread the almonds on a baking sheet and toast them in the oven, turning them occasionally, until they are dark brown. Chop them very fine or put them through a food chopper.

3. Mix the almonds with the maple syrup to make a thin paste, adding more maple syrup if it seems too thick.

4. Spoon a generous tablespoon of the almond paste into the bottoms of 6 to 8 parfait or wine glasses. Cover it with a thick layer of the ice cream. Continue in this manner until the glasses are full.

5. Cover the parfaits with plastic wrap and freeze until they are hard. Remove them from the freezer 30 minutes before serving and put them in the refrigerator. Top with whipped cream.

YIELD : 6 TO 8 SERVINGS

FRESH LIME SORBET

You may store this sorbet in the freezer as you would ice cream. Its tart flavor is delightfully refreshing.

> 1 cup sugar
> 3 cups water
> 1 cup fresh lime juice (6 to 8 juicy limes)
>   grated rind of 2 limes
> 2 drops green vegetable coloring
> 2 egg whites
>   sprigs of mint for decoration

1. Combine the sugar and water in a saucepan, bring the mixture to a boil, and simmer the syrup for 10 minutes. Let it cool.

2. Add the lime juice and rind and vegetable coloring to the syrup and pour the mixture into a refrigerator tray. Let the mixture cool and put it in the freezing compartment of the refrigerator for 1 hour.

3. Remove the tray from the freezing compartment, stir the mixture thoroughly to prevent ice granules from forming, and return it to the freezing compartment until it is the consistency of wet snow.

4. Beat the egg whites until they are stiff and fold them into the lime mixture. Pour the sorbet into chilled sorbet glasses and garnish each serving with a sprig of mint.

YIELD : 8 TO 10 SERVINGS

ICED GRENADINE SORBET

The secret of making this delicate pink sorbet lies in the mixing of the syrup, grenadine, and fruit juices while the mixture freezes. This keeps it free of ice particles and assures the proper consistency.

> $\frac{1}{4}$ cup sugar
> 1 cup water
> 1 cup grenadine
> 6 tablespoons lemon juice
> 2 tablespoons orange juice
> 2 egg whites

1. In a saucepan combine the sugar and water. Simmer the syrup for 5 minutes and let it cool.

2. Add to the cooled syrup the grenadine, lemon juice, and orange juice. Pour the mixture into a refrigerator tray and freeze it in the freezing compartment of the refrigerator, beating it from time to time with a fork.

3. Beat the egg whites until they hold definite peaks. Mix into the grenadine mixture, return the sorbet to the refrigerator tray and freeze it, turning the mixture from time to time to prevent the grenadine from falling to the bottom of the tray.

YIELD : 4 TO 6 SERVINGS

TORTONI

This celebrated Italian dessert is very easy to make. It can be stored in the freezer, covered, like ice cream. It should be moved from the freezer to the refrigerator 1 hour before serving.

> 1 cup heavy cream
> ¼ cup confectioners sugar
> 1 egg white
> 6 Italian macaroons
> 2 teaspoons Marsala or dry sherry
>   crushed macaroons and whipped cream for decoration
>   (optional)

1. Whip the cream and fold in the sugar.

2. Beat the egg white until stiff and fold it into the whipped cream.

3. Crush the macaroons and force them through a sieve.

4. Stir the macaroons and wine into the whipped cream mixture. Pour the mixture into 6 small paper cups or ramekins and freeze them. Sprinkle the tops with crushed macaroons and top them with whipped cream, if desired.

YIELD : 6 SERVINGS

COLD SOUFFLÉS

Cold Soufflés make splendid desserts, and they are not difficult to prepare. But there *are* pitfalls, and care must be taken to avoid them. When the soufflé base is made with egg yolks, it must not be allowed to overcook, or the result will be curdled scrambled eggs. If one is nervous, or making a soufflé for the first time, it helps to have a bowl of ice water by the stove. If the egg yolk and milk or cream mixture appears to be thickening too quickly, plunge the top of the double boiler into the water and stir the mixture briskly. This will stop the cooking immediately.

It is also important that the custard be cool when the whipped cream is added, or the cream will separate. And the cream must not be over-beaten, as the lightness of the soufflé depends in part on the lightness of the whipped cream.

The egg whites, too, must be handled with care. They should be folded into the mixture with a large metal spoon because its cutting edge is sharper than that of a wooden spoon or spatula, and therefore not as likely to break up the air bubbles and deflate the egg whites, which would result in a heavier soufflé. They should be folded in quickly and smoothly, the spoon being lifted from the bottom up the side of the bowl. And the egg whites should be beaten only at the last minute, or they will become flat. Finally, the gelatin must always be sprinkled over cold water to soften and dissolved over the lowest heat possible. Heat the water only until it is sufficiently warm to dissolve the powder.

ICED CHOCOLATE SOUFFLÉ

8 squares (8 ounces) semi-sweet chocolate
1 pint half and half
2 envelopes unflavored gelatin
$\frac{1}{4}$ cup cold water
6 eggs, separated
$\frac{1}{2}$ cup sugar
2 teaspoons vanilla
$\frac{1}{2}$ teaspoon salt
$\frac{1}{4}$ cup dark rum
1 pint heavy cream
  dry cake crumbs or crushed macaroons

1. Oil lightly the inside of a 1-quart soufflé mold. Fold over lengthwise a long strip of aluminum foil and oil it on one side. Tie it around the mold, oiled side in, to make a collar standing 3 inches above the top.

2. In the top of a double boiler over hot water melt the chocolate in the half and half.

3. Sprinkle the gelatin over the cold water to soften.

4. Beat the egg yolks with $\frac{1}{4}$ cup of the sugar until they are light and lemon-colored. To the chocolate mixture add the vanilla, salt, egg yolk mixture, and softened gelatin. Cook the mixture over hot water, stirring constantly, until it is the consistency of very heavy cream. Let it cool. Add the rum and chill the mixture until it begins to thicken.

5. Beat the cream with the remaining $\frac{1}{4}$ cup sugar until it is thick but not stiff.

6. Beat the egg whites until they hold firm peaks.

7. Combine the chocolate mixture with the whipped cream and fold in the egg whites with a large metal spoon. Spoon into the soufflé mold and chill for at least 3 hours.

8. Remove the collar before serving. Pat dry cake crumbs or crushed macaroons onto the sides of the dessert.

YIELD : 10 TO 12 SERVINGS

CHAPEL CLEEVE COLD LEMON SOUFFLÉ

I persevered with the cook at this famous English country house for months before she finally told me the correct ingredients and method for preparing this delicious dessert. (Giving a recipe incorrectly was considered the prerogative of old-time cooks, as recipes were guarded secrets.) It is reputed that, in the days when footmen were employed, this same cook always made an extra soufflé—to throw at the footman when he pestered her for the next course. Even the most devoted scale watchers break down when they are confronted with this lemon soufflé. It may be prepared well ahead of time.

1 envelope unflavored gelatin

$\frac{1}{4}$ cup water

$\frac{3}{4}$ cup cold milk

4 egg yolks

$\frac{1}{2}$ cup sugar

$\frac{1}{2}$ cup lemon juice

3 tablespoons grated lemon rind

1 cup heavy cream

7 egg whites

dry cake crumbs

1. Fold over lengthwise a long strip of aluminum foil and oil it on one side. Tie it neatly around a 1-quart soufflé dish mold, oiled side in, to make a collar standing 3 inches above the top.

2. Sprinkle the gelatin over the water to soften.

3. Heat the milk in the top of a double boiler. Beat the egg yolks with the sugar until they are light and lemon-colored and pour the hot milk over them. Return the mixture to the top of the double boiler and add the gelatin.

4. Cook the mixture over hot water, stirring or whisking constantly, until it is thick and creamy, being careful that it does not boil. Remove the pan from the heat, let the mixture cool (this is important to preserve the freshness of the lemon) and add the lemon juice and rind. Refrigerate the mixture until it begins to thicken. Keep a careful watch because you are in trouble if it sets solid.

5. Whip the cream until it is thick but not stiff, and fold it into the lemon custard mixture. Refrigerate the mixture until it is just beginning to set.

6. Beat the egg whites until they are stiff but not dry and fold them gently into the mixture with a large metal spoon. Spoon the soufflé into the prepared mold and chill it for at least 3 hours, or longer.

7. Remove the collar before serving and pat dry cake crumbs over the side. In the days of hourglass waists when Edward VII was the social leader of Europe, candied violets and rosettes decorated the top.

YIELD : 6 TO 8 SERVINGS

ICED COFFEE SOUFFLÉ

This strongly flavored coffee dessert is prepared in exactly the same manner as the Iced Chocolate Soufflé.

   1 envelope unflavored gelatin
   $\frac{1}{4}$ cup water
   1$\frac{1}{2}$ cups milk
   3 egg yolks
   $\frac{1}{2}$ cup sugar
   8 tablespoons instant coffee
   2 tablespoons brandy
   1 cup heavy cream
   5 egg whites
      macaroon or cake crumbs

1. Oil lightly a 1-quart soufflé mold. Fold over lengthwise a long strip of aluminum foil and oil it on one side. Tie it around the mold, oiled side in, to make a collar standing 3 inches above the top.

2. Soften the gelatin by sprinkling it over the water.

3. Heat the milk in the top of a double boiler over hot but not boiling water. Beat the egg yolks with the sugar and pour the milk over them. Return the mixture to the top of the double boiler, add the softened gelatin, and whisk in the coffee, 1 tablespoon at a time. Cook the mixture, whisking constantly, until it is the consistency of heavy cream. Let it cool and stir in the brandy.

4. Whip the cream until it is thick but not stiff and fold it into the mixture. Refrigerate the mixture until it begins to set.

5. Beat the egg whites until they are stiff but not dry and fold them into the mixture. Spoon it into the prepared mold and chill it for at least 3 hours.

6. To serve, remove foil and pat macaroon or cake crumbs on the sides of the dessert.

YIELD : 8 TO 10 SERVINGS

ICED GRENADINE SOUFFLÉ

A delightful pale pink dessert with a distinct almond flavor, this soufflé is strongly recommended to those with a sweet tooth.

>1 envelope unflavored gelatin
>$\frac{1}{4}$ cup cold water
>4 eggs, separated
>$\frac{1}{2}$ cup sugar
>$\frac{1}{4}$ teaspoon salt
>$\frac{1}{2}$ cup grenadine
>1 cup grated unblanched almonds
>$\frac{1}{2}$ teaspoon almond extract
> juice of 1 lemon
>1 cup heavy cream
> macaroon or cake crumbs

1. Lightly oil a 1-quart soufflé mold. Fold over lengthwise a long strip of aluminum foil and oil it on one side. Tie it around the mold, oiled side in, to make a collar standing 3 inches above the top.

2. Sprinkle the gelatin over the water to soften.

3. Put the egg yolks in the top of a double boiler. Stir in the sugar, salt, and softened gelatin and cook the mixture over gently boiling water, whisking constantly or beating with a rotary beater, until it is slightly thick and custardy. Remove it from the heat and stir in the grenadine, almonds, almond extract, and lemon juice. Let the mixture cool.

4. Beat the cream until it is thick but not stiff and mix it into the cool custard.

5. Beat the egg whites until they stand in peaks and fold them gently into the mixture.

6. Spoon the soufflé mixture into the prepared mold (it will fill it to the brim) and refrigerate it until it is spongy and firm.

7. To serve, remove the foil and pat macaroon or cake crumbs on the sides of the soufflé rising above the mold.

YIELD : 4 TO 6 SERVINGS

SOUFFLÉ MONTE CRISTO

An exotic dessert, and not nearly as fattening as it sounds. The combination of bitter chocolate, kirsch, and fresh strawberries is unusual and exciting. If a tall, narrow glass is not available, a beer can with both ends removed makes a good substitute. Make the soufflé the day before and decorate it just before serving. This dessert was given to me by Odette Bery and is one of her favorites.

> 4 large egg yolks
> $\frac{1}{3}$ cup sugar
> 1 envelope unflavored gelatin
> $\frac{1}{4}$ cup water
> 4 to 6 tablespoons kirsch
> 1 cup heavy cream
> 5 large egg whites
> 2 squares (2 ounces) unsweetened chocolate, grated
> 1 pint fresh strawberries
> sugar
> sweetened whipped cream for decoration

1. Lightly oil a 1-quart soufflé dish or mold. Fold over lengthwise a long strip of aluminum foil and oil it on one side. Tie it around the mold, oiled side in, to make a collar standing 3 inches above the top.

2. Oil the outside of a tall, narrow glass and place it in the center of the mold.

3. Beat the egg yolks with the $\frac{1}{3}$ cup sugar until they are thick and lemon-colored.

4. Sprinkle the gelatin over the water, let it stand for 10 minutes, and dissolve it over gentle heat, but do not let it boil. Stir it into the egg yolk mixture and stir in the kirsch.

5. Whip the cream until it is thick but not stiff and fold it into the egg-yolk mixture.

6. Beat the egg whites until they are stiff and fold them into the mixture. Pour half of it into the prepared soufflé mold, being careful not to get any in the glass, and sprinkle it with the grated chocolate. Pour in the remaining soufflé mixture. It should come $\frac{1}{2}$ inch above the dish. Refrigerate the soufflé for at least 4 hours.

7. Wash the strawberries or wipe them with a damp cloth. Hull them and sprinkle them with sugar and kirsch to taste.

8. Remove the foil collar from the mold. Gently run a knife around the glass and carefully remove it. Fill the cavity immediately with the strawberries, packing them in tightly, reserving a few for decoration.

9. Garnish the soufflé with rosettes of sweetened whipped cream and strawberries cut in quarters.

YIELD : 6 SERVINGS

ST. JOHN'S ICED LIME SOUFFLÉ

This is one of the most delicious desserts I know. The color, texture and flavor cannot be beaten.

> 1 envelope unflavored gelatin
> $\frac{1}{4}$ cup water
> $\frac{3}{4}$ cup milk
> 4 egg yolks
> $\frac{1}{2}$ cup sugar
> $\frac{1}{2}$ cup fresh lime juice (approximately 6 limes)
> 1 cup heavy cream
> 3 drops green food coloring
> 7 egg whites

1. Oil lightly a 1-quart soufflé mold. Fold over lengthwise a long strip of aluminum foil and oil it on one side. Tie it around the mold, oiled side in, to make a collar standing 3 inches above the top.

2. Sprinkle the gelatin over the water to soften.

3. Heat the milk in the top of a double boiler. Beat the egg yolks with the sugar until they are light and lemon-colored and pour the hot milk over them. Return the mixture to the top of the double boiler and add the gelatin.

4. Cook the mixture over hot water, stirring or whisking constantly, until it is thick and creamy, being careful that it does not boil. Remove the pan from the heat, let the mixture cool, and add the lime juice. Refrigerate the mixture until it begins to thicken.

5. Whip the cream until it is thick but not stiff and fold it into the lime mixture, adding 3 drops *only* of green food coloring. Refrigerate the mixture until it is just beginning to set.

6. Beat the egg whites until they are stiff but not dry and fold them gently into the mixture with a metal spoon. Spoon the soufflé into the prepared mold and chill it for at least 3 hours or longer if desired.

YIELD : 6 TO 8 SERVINGS

SUMMER PUDDING

As the name indicates, this is a seasonal dessert. Although frozen red currants and raspberries may be substituted for the fresh fruit, the result is not nearly as good. Few desserts can be as refreshing and delightful as this pudding on a hot summer day. This is as English as John Bull.

> 6 to 8 thin slices white bread
> 4 cups raspberries
> 4 cups red currants
> 1 tablespoon water
> 1 cup sugar
> 1 cup heavy cream
> $\frac{1}{4}$ cup sugar

1. Line the bottom and sides of a 2-quart mixing bowl with the bread slices, shaping the slices against the bowl. Reserve enough bread to cover the top of the pudding.

2. In a heavy pan combine the raspberries, currants, water, and the 1 cup sugar. Cook the mixture for 2 minutes and let it cool. Pour it into the bread-lined bowl and cover it with the reserved bread slices. Cover the top with a plate and put a weight on top of the plate. Chill the pudding overnight.

3. Unmold the pudding on a serving platter. Whip the cream stiffly, flavor it with the $\frac{1}{4}$ cup sugar, and serve it with the pudding.

YIELD : 6 TO 8 SERVINGS

JANUARY PUDDING

This dessert was always made specially for me when I happened to be home for my birthday. The recipe comes from my grandmother's kitchen, and I've never seen or heard of a pudding like it elsewhere. It is a perfect dish for cold weather. If put on the stove to steam after breakfast, it will be ready in time for luncheon. Young people love it.

$\frac{1}{2}$ cup (1 stick) sweet butter
$\frac{1}{2}$ cup brown sugar
2 eggs, lightly beaten
2 heaping tablespoons raspberry jam
1 cup flour
$\frac{1}{2}$ teaspoon baking soda
Raspberry Jam Sauce (*see below*)
Custard Sauce (*see below*)

1. Cream the butter with the sugar. Mix in the eggs and jam.

2. Sift together the flour and baking soda. Fold it quickly into the jam mixture. Spoon the mixture into a greased 1-quart steaming mold and steam it for at least 2 hours (a little longer won't hurt).

3. Serve the pudding hot with Raspberry Jam Sauce or Custard Sauce.

Raspberry Jam Sauce

$\frac{1}{2}$ cup raspberry jam
$\frac{1}{4}$ cup water
juice of 1 lemon

Dissolve the raspberry jam in the water and lemon juice over low heat.

Custard Sauce

4 egg yolks
$\frac{1}{2}$ cup sugar
1 teaspoon vanilla
2 cups milk

1. Combine the egg yolks with the sugar and vanilla and beat the mixture until it is creamy.

2. Bring the milk to a boil and very gradually pour it over the egg yolk mixture, whisking constantly.

3. Pour the custard into the top of a double boiler and cook it over hot water, stirring constantly, until it is thick.

YIELD : 6 SERVINGS

QUEEN'S PUDDING

This pudding has been attributed to England's unfortunate and most maligned Queen Charlotte. It is an example of English country cooking, and not nearly as fattening as one would suppose. It may be served hot, cold, or at room temperature, which I prefer.

> 2 cups milk
> ½ cup sugar
> 1 teaspoon vanilla
> rind of 1 lemon, cut into matchsticks
> 1½ cups fresh white bread crumbs, freshly grated
> 1 whole egg
> 3 eggs, separated
> ¼ cup raspberry jam
> pinch of salt
> 3 tablespoons sugar

1. Preheat the oven to 350°F.

2. In a saucepan heat the milk, the ½ cup sugar, vanilla, and lemon rind. Stir in the bread crumbs. Remove the pan from the heat. Lightly beat the egg and egg yolks and stir into the milk mixture.

3. Pour the mixture into a 1-quart ovenproof dish and bake it in the oven until the custard is set and lightly browned. Remove it from the oven and spread it with the jam.

4. Raise the oven temperature to 500°F.

5. Whip the egg whites with the salt until they hold soft peaks. Add the 3 tablespoons sugar, 1 tablespoon at a time, and continue to beat the whites until they are stiff.

6. Spread the meringue over the pudding and bake it in the oven for about 5 minutes, or until the meringue is browned.

YIELD : 6 SERVINGS

ELIZA FURY'S ESSEX ALMOND PUDDING

Eliza Fury was my cook in England. She was without formal education, but spent much of her spare time visiting museums, and she knew more about antiques than anyone I've ever met. Above all, she was a natural

and marvelous cook. This rich and delicious pudding is best when prepared the day before it is to be served. The directions must be followed
exactly.

> 12 to 14 ladyfingers, halved
> ½ cup (1 stick) sweet butter
> ½ cup sugar
> 2 cups finely ground almonds
> 1 teaspoon almond extract
> 2 eggs
> whipped cream, candied violets, and angelica for decoration

1. Put the ladyfingers in a very slow oven (225°F.) until they are dry.

2. Line a 1-quart bowl or mold with strips of wax paper. These are used
   to lift the pudding out of the bowl. Line the bowl with the ladyfingers, reserving a few for the top.

3. In a bowl cream the butter and sugar. Mix in the almonds and
   almond extract and add the eggs, one at a time, mixing thoroughly
   after each addition. Spoon the mixture into the prepared bowl and
   cover the top with the reserved ladyfingers. Place a small plate on
   top and a heavy weight on top of that. Refrigerate the pudding for at
   least 24 hours.

4. Turn out the pudding on a cake stand, using the strips of wax paper
   as handles. Decorate it with whipped cream, candied violets, and
   angelica. This makes ten servings, but I've often known the pudding
   to look very much diminished after a meal for eight.

YIELD : 8 TO 10 SERVINGS

YORKSHIRE TRIFLE

> 12 to 14 ladyfingers, halved
> 1–inch layer of stale sponge cake
> 12–ounce jar black raspberry jam
> 10 to 12 Italian macaroons, crushed
> 1 cup Madeira wine
> 2 cups milk
> 6 egg yolks
> ½ cup sugar
> grated rind of 1 lemon

$\frac{1}{4}$ teaspoon salt
4 tablespoons brandy
$\frac{1}{2}$ teaspoon vanilla
$\frac{1}{2}$ teaspoon lemon extract
3 tablespoons kirsch
2 tablespoons white wine
2 cups heavy cream
$\frac{1}{4}$ cup sugar
slivered almonds and candied cherries for decoration

1. Line the sides of a 1$\frac{1}{2}$- to 2-quart cut glass or china bowl with the halved ladyfingers, standing them upright, the flat sides against the sides of the bowl. Cover the bottom of the bowl with the sponge cake, spread the cake with the jam, and cover the jam with the crushed macaroons. Pour on the Madeira and refrigerate the bowl.

2. Make a boiled custard : Scald the milk in a saucepan. Beat the egg yolks and combine them with the $\frac{1}{2}$ cup sugar, the lemon rind, and the salt. Slowly add the scalded milk, stirring constantly. Pour the mixture into the top of a double boiler and cook it over hot but not boiling water, stirring constantly, until it is thick enough to coat a spoon. Let the custard cool.

3. Add the brandy and vanilla to the cooled custard. Beat the mixture well and refrigerate it.

4. In a glass bowl set in a bowl of cracked ice, mix together the lemon extract, kirsch, white wine, cream and $\frac{1}{4}$ cup sugar. Whip the mixture until it is stiff and refrigerate it for 2 hours.

5. To assemble the trifle, pour the custard over the jam and cake in the bowl and pour the whipped cream mixture over the custard. Sprinkle the top with the slivered almonds and decorate the trifle with the candied cherries.

YIELD : 10 TO 14 SERVINGS

ORANGE BAVARIAN CREAM

This is a delightfully rich dessert—definitely not for weight-watchers. As with all Bavarian creams, care must be taken while unmolding. Dip the mold in hot water for 30 seconds and invert it over the serving platter. If it does not come out easily, cover the mold with a clean towel dipped in hot water and wrung dry. Repeat if necessary.

1 cup milk
grated rind of 1 orange
3 egg yolks
½ cup sugar
juice of ½ orange
1 envelope unflavored gelatin
1 cup heavy cream
whipped cream, orange slices, and pitted cherries for
decoration

1. In a saucepan heat the milk with the grated orange rind.

2. In a large bowl beat the egg yolks with the sugar and orange juice. Strain the milk and add it to the egg-yolk mixture. Cook the mixture over low heat, stirring constantly, until it is thickened.

3. Remove the mixture from the heat and stir in the gelatin. Strain the mixture, let it cool, and refrigerate it until it is just beginning to set.

4. Whip the cream until it stands in peaks and fold it gently but thoroughly into the orange mixture. Pour the Bavarian cream into a moistened charlotte mold or ring mold and chill it for at least 3 hours.

5. Unmold the dessert on a platter and decorate it with whipped cream, orange slices, and cherries.

YIELD : 8 TO 10 SERVINGS

CHOCOLATE BAVARIAN CREAM

Apply exactly the same care and principles as you would in preparing Orange Bavarian Cream.

6 squares (6 ounces) sweet cooking chocolate, broken into small
pieces, or 1 package (6 ounces) semi-sweet chocolate bits
2 cups milk
2 envelopes unflavored gelatin
½ cup cold water
4 egg yolks
¼ cup sugar
2 cups heavy cream
3 tablespoons sugar
whipped cream and candied violets for decoration

1. In a saucepan combine the chocolate and milk. Heat the mixture over moderate heat, stirring constantly, until the chocolate is melted.

2. Soften the gelatin by sprinkling it over the water.

3. In a large bowl combine the egg yolks with the ¼ cup sugar and beat the mixture with an electric or rotary beater for 5 minutes. Gradually stir in the chocolate mixture. Pour the mixture into the top of a double boiler, add the softened gelatin, and cook over simmering water, stirring constantly with a wooden spoon, until it begins to thicken and coats the back of the spoon. Refrigerate the mixture until it begins to get stiff.

4. Beat the cream with the 3 tablespoons sugar until it stands in peaks. With a spatula fold it gently but thoroughly into the chocolate mixture. Pour the Bavarian cream into a 6-cup mold and refrigerate it for several hours, or until it is firm.

5. Unmold the dessert on a platter and garnish it with whipped cream, piped into rosettes, and candied violets.

YIELD : 8 TO 10 SERVINGS

CHOCOLATE MOUSSE

Chocolate is a flavor that few can resist, and this is one of the best chocolate mousses I know. It is also quick and easy to prepare—a matter of 10 minutes. The addition of butter eliminates the headache of the chocolate's becoming hard before the egg white can be folded in. This mousse can be prepared well ahead of time and the recipe can be successfully doubled, tripled, *ad infinitum*.

> 1 square (1 ounce) semi-sweet chocolate
> 1 teaspoon sweet butter
> 1 egg, separated
> 1 teaspoon sugar
> ¼ teaspoon vanilla or rum

1. In the top of a double boiler melt the chocolate with the butter. Cool slightly. Beat the egg yolk and stir into the chocolate mixture.

2. Whip the egg white with the sugar until it is stiff.

3. Fold beaten egg white and vanilla or rum gently but thoroughly into the chocolate mixture.

4. Spoon the mousse into a glass dish or ramekin and chill for at least 2 hours before serving.

YIELD : 1 SERVING

HOT LEMON SOUFFLÉ

This is light as a feather and simple to put together. Have no fear of serving it after the richest of entrées.

      6 egg yolks
      ½ cup sugar
        pinch salt
        grated rind and juice of 2 lemons (½ cup juice)
      7 egg whites
        pinch cream of tartar
     sprinkling of confectioners' sugar

1. Preheat oven to 375°F.

2. Beat the egg yolks till they are thick and light yellow. Gradually add the sugar and salt and continue beating until mixture is smooth. Beat in the lemon rind and juice.

3. Whip the egg whites. When they reach the foamy stage add the cream of tartar and continue beating until they hold definite peaks.

4. Fold the beaten egg whites into the yolk mixture gently but thoroughly. Start off by mixing in two spoonfuls of egg white, and continue by folding.

5. Spoon into a 2-quart soufflé dish and place the dish in a pan of boiling water. The water should reach ¾ of the way up the dish. Bake for 35 to 40 minutes.

6. Sprinkle with confectioners' sugar and serve immediately.

YIELD : 6 TO 8 SERVINGS

APRICOT SOUFFLÉ

      1 cup dried apricots (tightly packed)
      ¼ cup sugar
      3 egg whites
        pinch cream of tartar

$\frac{1}{3}$ cup sugar

$\frac{1}{2}$ teaspoon almond extract

whipped cream

1. Soak the dried apricots overnight in sufficient water to cover. Cook the apricots slowly, covered, until tender. If the water boils away, add a little more. Add the $\frac{1}{4}$ cup sugar and cook for 2 minutes, stirring. Cool, force through a wire strainer, and reserve. Purée should be heavy and not liquid or runny. You will have a little more than the half cup required. Reserve.

2. Butter the inside of a bowl or mold, and sprinkle evenly with sugar, shaking out the surplus. If a lid is being used, repeat this step on the lid. If a bowl is being used do the same to a piece of wax paper large enough to tie over the bowl in place of a lid. If you own a 2-quart double boiler, it is ideal for cooking the soufflé. Have a pan of boiling water ready. The water should be sufficient to come $\frac{2}{3}$ of the way up the bowl or mold.

3. Beat the egg whites till frothing. Add cream of tartar and continue beating till soft peaks are formed. Add the $\frac{1}{3}$ cup sugar gradually and continue beating till stiff. Add the almond extract.

4. Fold the egg white mixture into $\frac{1}{2}$ cup reserved apricot purée with a large metal spoon and spoon into the mold or bowl. Tie wax paper securely over the bowl, or cover mold with lid.

5. Place the mold in the boiling water and reduce heat till just simmering. Cook for 40 minutes. Add more water to pan if required.

6. Turn out on a warm serving platter and serve whipped cream separately. This soufflé will wait for you up to 15 or 20 minutes.

NOTE: Doubling the quantity is very successful and will serve 8 generously.

YIELD : 4 TO 6 SERVINGS

CHOCOLATE SANDWICH

I have served this exotic dessert to old and young, male and female, and have found it to be a favorite with all. The flavor of anise is elusive and unusual.

Cake

    3 eggs, separated

    5 tablespoons sugar

    3 tablespoons cocoa

    1 teaspoon vanilla

    ½ teaspoon almond extract

    ½ teaspoon cinnamon

    ½ teaspoon ground anise

Filling

    1½ cups heavy cream

    ¼ cup sugar

    4 tablespoons cocoa

    ½ teaspoon vanilla

    2 tablespoons chopped toasted pistachio nuts for decoration

1. Preheat the oven to 350°F. Oil an 8- or 9-inch square cake pan and carefully line it with wax paper.

2. In a bowl beat the egg yolks thoroughly with a rotary or electric beater. Gradually add the sugar and continue beating the mixture until it is very creamy. Stir in the cocoa, vanilla, almond extract, cinnamon, and anise.

3. Beat the egg whites until they hold definite peaks. Fold in the cocoa mixture very gently.

4. Pour the batter into the prepared pan and bake it for 25 minutes, or until the cake pulls away from the sides of the pan. Cool the cake for 5 minutes, remove it from the pan, and peel off the wax paper. Let the cake cool completely.

5. Make the filling: In a bowl mix together the cream, sugar, cocoa, and vanilla. Chill the mixture for 1 to 2 hours.

6. Beat the filling until it holds a shape. Cut the cake in half horizontally. Spread one layer with one-third of the filling and sandwich the two halves together. Put the remaining filling in a pastry bag and pipe rosettes of it over the top of the cake. Sprinkle with the pistachio nuts.

YIELD : 4 TO 6 SERVINGS

BABA AU RHUM

This is the classic French method for making baba au rhum.

1 envelope yeast
$\frac{1}{4}$ cup lukewarm water
3 tablespoons sugar
$\frac{1}{2}$ teaspoon salt
$\frac{1}{4}$ cup lukewarm milk
4 eggs, lightly beaten
2 cups sifted flour
$\frac{2}{3}$ cup soft sweet butter
1 tablespoon Sultana raisins
1 tablespoon currants
2 cups water
1 cup sugar
$\frac{1}{2}$ cup dark rum
$\frac{3}{4}$ cup apricot preserves
candied cherries or whole blanched almonds for decoration

1. Preheat oven to 350°F.

2. Sprinkle the yeast over the lukewarm water to soften. Combine it in a bowl with the 3 tablespoons sugar, salt, milk, and eggs. Stir in the flour and beat the dough hard with a wooden spoon for at least 8 minutes. Cover the bowl with a tea towel, set it in a warm spot, and let the dough rise until it is double in bulk.

3. Beat in the butter, raisins, and currants until the butter is completely incorporated.

4. Grease baba molds or muffin tins and fill about one-third full with the dough and let the babas rise until they are almost double in bulk.

5. Bake the babas for 20 to 25 minutes, or until a toothpick inserted in the center comes out dry.

6. Unmold the babas onto a shallow dish with a rim and let them cool slightly.

7. Make a syrup. In a saucepan bring to a boil the 2 cups water and

1 cup sugar. Remove the pan from the heat, let the syrup cool to lukewarm, and stir in the rum.

8. Prick the tops of the babas in several places with a toothpick and gradually pour the syrup over them. Let them stand for about 30 minutes, basting them frequently with the syrup.

9. Heat the apricot preserves, work them through a sieve, and spoon or brush over the babas. Decorate each baba with a candied cherry or whole blanched almond.

YIELD : 15 TO 20 SERVINGS

BARBARA CROUCH'S ANGEL FOOD CAKE

This recipe was given to me by a kind and generous friend who claims that she hates to cook. But she is actually quite painstaking in the kitchen. This cake may be varied by using half flour and half cocoa. It is the most successful angel food recipe I know. Follow the directions carefully.

1 cup sifted flour
1½ cups sugar
¼ teaspoon salt
9 egg whites
1 teaspoon cream of tartar
1½ teaspoons vanilla

1. Preheat the oven to 350°F. Sift the flour 5 times. Sift the sugar 5 times.

2. Add the salt to the egg whites and beat them until they are frothy. Sprinkle on the cream of tartar and continue to beat the whites until soft peaks form. Sprinkle on the sugar, 4 tablespoons at a time. After each addition fold in the sugar with a spoon, never letting the spoon rise above the surface of the mixture.

3. Fold in the flour in the same manner, adding the vanilla with the last of the flour.

4. Pour the batter into a 10-inch ungreased tube pan. Break any air bubbles with a knife. Bake the cake in the oven for 30 minutes.

5. Invert the pan on a cake rack, let the cake cool completely and unmold it on a cake stand.

YIELD : 10 TO 12 SERVINGS

BASIC PASTRY

> 2 cups flour
> ½ teaspoon salt
> ½ cup (1 stick) sweet butter
> 3 tablespoons vegetable shortening
> 2½ to 3 tablespoons cold water

1. Blend all the ingredients, except water, with a pastry cutter or knife. Gradually add the water, as little as possible, but sufficient to bind.

2. On a pastry board, knead with the heel of the hand, starting from the outside, and pressing hard. Form into a ball, wrap, and chill for at least 2 hours before rolling out.

BAKED PIE SHELL

1. Preheat oven to 400°F.

2. Roll Basic Pastry to ⅛ inch thick.

3. Line a 9-inch pie dish. Trim pastry and prick with a fork, and bake 15 to 20 minutes.

LEMON MERINGUE PIE

The lemon filling in this pie is made from an old recipe and bears no resemblance to the version now generally accepted. It is rich, creamy, and excitingly fresh. When you've tasted this filling you will be dissatisfied with all others.

> 9-inch Baked Pie Shell (*see preceding recipe*)

Lemon Filling

> 3 eggs
> 1 egg yolk
> 1 cup sugar
> 1 stick (½ cup) butter
> juice and grated rind of 1 lemon

Meringue

> 5 egg whites
> $\frac{1}{2}$ teaspoon salt
> $\frac{1}{4}$ teaspoon cream of tartar
> 1 teaspoon vanilla
> $1\frac{1}{2}$ tablespoons superfine sugar

1. Make the filling. In the top of a double boiler combine the eggs, egg yolk, and sugar. Stir in the butter and the lemon juice and rind. Cook the mixture over hot water, stirring constantly, until it is thick, making sure that it does not boil. Let the filling cool and pour it into the baked pie shell.

2. Heat the oven to 500°F.

3. Make the meringue. Beat the egg whites with the salt until they are foamy. Sprinkle them with the cream of tartar and add the vanilla and half the sugar. Continue beating the egg whites until they are stiff. Fold in the rest of the sugar.

4. Spoon the meringue over the lemon filling and roughen the top with a spatula, or force meringue through a pastry bag. Bake the pie until the meringue is lightly browned, approximately 5 minutes.

YIELD : 6 TO 8 SERVINGS

APPLE TART

> 5 or 6 apples (Delicious or Greening)
>   strip of lemon peel
> $\frac{1}{4}$ teaspoon cinnamon
>   sugar to taste
> 9–inch Baked Pie Shell (*see page* 152)
> 3 tablespoons apricot jam
> 2 tablespoons sugar
>   confectioners' sugar

1. Preheat oven to 400°F.

2. Peel and core the apples. Chop 3 of them and place in a saucepan. Add 2 tablespoons of water and the lemon peel. Cook until soft. Add the cinnamon and sugar to taste. Beat until smooth.

3. Spread the apple purée evenly over the bottom of the baked pie shell.

4. Slice the remaining apples very thin. Starting from the outside of the pie shell, lay them in a circle, each one overlapping the other. Place in the oven and bake for 20 minutes.

5. Combine the apricot jam, 2 tablespoons sugar and 2 tablespoons of water in a saucepan and cook slowly for 10 minutes. Rub the mixture through a fine sieve to remove lumps. Brush the apricot purée over the apples and cool.

6. Before serving, dust the surface of the tart lightly with confectioners' sugar.

YIELD : 4 TO 6 SERVINGS

FRESH PEACH TART

> 7 or 8 fresh ripe peaches
> sugar (optional)
> 9–inch Baked Pie Shell (*see page* 152)
> 3 tablespoons apricot jam
> 2 tablespoons sugar
> superfine sugar

1. Dip the peaches into boiling water for 1 minute, and then remove the skins.

2. Chop 4 of the peaches into a saucepan, add 1 tablespoon of water, and cook slowly until soft. Beat into a purée, adding sugar, if necessary.

3. Spread the purée evenly on the bottom of the pie shell.

4. Cut the remaining peaches into thin slices. Starting from the outside of the pie shell, lay them in a circle, each one overlapping the other.

5. Combine the apricot jam, 2 tablespoons sugar, and 2 tablespoons of water in a saucepan, and cook slowly for 10 minutes. Rub the mixture through a fine sieve to remove lumps. Brush the purée evenly over the peach slices.

6. Before serving, dust the surface of the tart lightly with superfine sugar.

YIELD : 4 TO 6 SERVINGS

MENUS FOR OCCASIONS

PARTIES and campaigns have much in common, the most obvious element being the careful planning required to guarantee success. Substitute enemy for guests or guests for enemy, depending on how you approach either event, and the operation takes on force and meaning.

I select guests for their differences, not their similarities, but draw the line by not inviting lifelong enemies to sit at the same table. A pot pourri of guests is stimulating.

Having decided on the number of guests one can have with comfort, choose the menu with great care, paying particular attention to what can be done in your kitchen and what you are confident of doing well—unless you are one of the few fortunates who have a cook.

Rarely do I have two hot courses, unless the occasion is a buffet. Usually the first course and last course are cold, and the main course and its accompaniments hot. Occasionally I serve salad and cheese as a separate course between the entrée and dessert. In this volume I have included many salads that are good as first courses. In fact, they are appetizers and often do away with having to serve a salad later.

Look for flavor, texture, and color when planning menus. If possible, avoid two rich creamy sauces in the same meal and remember that the shortest route to the stomach is through the eye. If you are serving wine, serve light wines first and follow up with fuller-bodied types.

I am partial to a round or oval table and am fortunate in having one of each. Both are conducive to conviviality and the conversation fairly flows. The dining table should be immaculate; silver, glass, and wood sparkling and linen spotless and crisp. Keep the decorations simple so as not to distract from the food and guests. If there are candles and flowers, the former should be high so as not to shine in the eye and the latter sufficiently low so as to allow an uninterrupted view of the other guests.

Do not bite off more than you can chew, or cook. It is far better to do one dish well than three poorly. Avoid last-minute chores so that you will be cool, calm and collected by the time your guests arrive. The harassment of a host or hostess is contagious. Brillat-Savarin says, "When you invite a man to dinner never forget that during the short time he is under your roof his happiness is in your hands." I would like to add, make certain those hands are cool.

One last word of advice. If you are helping guests to dishes, please, please make the helpings small. Nothing will kill an appetite as fast as the sight of a plate piled high with food.

MENUS

In this collection of menus you will find more for luncheons than either for dinners or buffet. If you wish to use a rather light luncheon menu for dinner, all that is needed is one extra dish of your choice.

The salads I choose for buffets are usually the non-wilt type. Delicate tossed greens are troublesome because the salad should be prepared and served and not allowed to stand. When it stands for any length of time on a buffet it assumes the appearance of wet, green Kleenex. The hard or "winter" salads look appetizing for hours. Don't be misled by the term "winter." These can be made just as easily in the summer and are suitable at any time of the year.

Luncheon menus are comparatively simple and light. Desserts have been included. Often you will find that fresh fruit and cheese are suggested. When buying fruit for dessert make sure it is ripe enough to serve and don't be misled by appearance. Often pears and peaches look good enough to eat when in fact they are as hard as bullets.

Dinner menus are more elaborate but are by no means beyond the capabilities of the average cook. Caviar has been suggested as a first course for one of the menus. If you can't afford to serve a lot don't select this menu for your party. One must be generous to the point of almost overdoing it with caviar.

Buffets are usually made up of dishes that can be eaten with a fork, but you will find some that need a knife also. These should be included only when you have sitting space and tables, large or small, available.

Play with the dishes as you would with bits of a jigsaw puzzle and soon you will be quite at ease with fitting them into their proper places. Remember the three important ingredients of a good menu : flavor, color, and texture, in pleasing combinations.

LUNCHEON

Saumon en Papillote
Potato Purée   Broccoli with Hollandaise Sauce

·

Friar's Omelet

Panache

·

Endive and Beet Salad

·

Lemon Meringue Pie

Chick Pea Salad
Crusty French or Italian Bread   Cheese

·

Baba au Rhum

Lobster Mousse
Green Beans with Water Chestnuts

·

St. John's Iced Lime Soufflé

Salmon Mousse in Aspic

·

Zucchini, Celery, and Mushrooms

·

Tortoni

Oysters Espagnol
Crusty French or Italian Bread   Cheese

·

Compote of Fruits

Blanquette de Veau
Spinach en Branche or Creamed Spinach

·

Fruit   Cheese

Sole Meunière
Potatoes Parisienne   Green Beans Vinaigrette

·

Frozen Bombe

Shrimp Newburg
Spinach Salad

·

Iced Chocolate Soufflé

Salmon Mousse in Aspic
Green Salad
Crusty French or Italian Bread   Cheese

·

Summer Pudding

Bouillabaise
Crusty French or Italian Bread

·

Apricot Soufflé

Sole Véronique
Spinach en Branche

·

Iced Coffee Soufflé

Poached Salmon
Small Boiled Potatoes   Green Salad

·

Soufflé Monte Cristo

Seafood Crêpes
Artichokes with Mustard Sauce

.

Orange Caramel

Escalopes de Veau
Sliced Tomato Salad   Vinaigrette Dressing

.

Compote of Fruits

Filet of Sole in Foil
Creamed Spinach

.

Hot Lemon Soufflé

Irish Stew
Green Salad

.

January Pudding

Lamb Chops Rouennaise
Tomatoes Stuffed with Potato Purée   Cold Green Beans
Vinaigrette Dressing

.

Soufflé Monte Cristo

Roast Rack of Lamb
Duchess Potatoes
Zucchini, Celery, and Mushrooms
Green Salad

.

Apple Tart

Curry of Lamb
Rice   Condiments

.

Chapel Cleeve Cold Lemon Soufflé

Braised Beef
Noodles   Spinach Salad
.
Chocolate Bavarian Cream

Quenelles de Brochet
.
Green Salad   Cheese
.
Compote of Fruits

Soufflé of Sole and Shrimp
Cold Green Beans   Vinaigrette Dressing
.
Summer Pudding

Braised Beef
Green Rice   Brussels Sprouts with Chestnuts
.
Orange Bavarian Cream

Meat Loaf de Luxe
Winter Salad
.
Tortoni

Blanquette de Veau
Shell Noodles   Cold Green Beans   Vinaigrette Dressing
.
Chocolate Mousse

Virginia Baked Chicken
Winter Salad
.
Yorkshire Trifle

Curry of Chicken
Rice   Condiments   Tomato Salad

.

Raspberry Fool

Gnocchi Parisienne
Endive and Beet Salad

.

St. John's Iced Lime Soufflé

Chicken Breasts with Green Olives
Potato Purée   Winter Salad

.

Sabayon Frappé

Sea Harvest
Saffron Rice   Green Salad

.

Fresh Peach Tart

Homard à l'Armoricaine
Green Rice   Green Salad

.

Fresh Fruit   Cheese

Kegeree
Spinach Salad

.

Apple Tart

Curry of Beef
Rice   Condiments

.

Fresh Fruit

Cottage Pie
Carrots, Celery, and Green Beans

.

Tortoni

Steak, Kidney and Oyster Pie
Carrots, Celery, and Green Beans

Fresh Lime Sorbet

Braised Tongue
Tomatoes Stuffed with Potato Purée
Green Salad

·

Toasted Almond Parfait

Poulet Normande
Brussels Sprouts with Chestnuts

Angel Food Cake   Strawberries

Chicken 243
Green Rice   Carrots Vichy
Green Salad

·

St. John's Iced Lime Soufflé

Chicken Breasts in Champagne Sauce
Green Rice   Winter Salad

·

Lemon Meringue Pie

Capon with Sauce Suprême
Potato Purée   Green Beans with Water Chestnuts

·

Apricot Soufflé

Nancy's Chicken
Winter Salad

·

Toasted Almond Parfait

Seafood Crêpes
Green Salad

·

Orange Caramel

Champignons sous Cloche
Green Salad   French Bread

Fresh Sliced Peaches

Ratatouille
French Bread   Cheese

·

Fresh Lime Sorbet

Deviled Crab   Tomatoes Provençale
Green Salad

·

Fresh Strawberries or Raspberries

Creamed Smoked Haddock
Tomato Salad   Vinaigrette Dressing

·

Chapel Cleeve Cold Lemon Soufflé

Quiche au Crabe
Summer Squash and Plum Tomatoes

·

Raspberry Fool

Mousse of Ham
Green Salad

·

Apple Tart

Egg Mousse
Cauliflower and Beet Salad

·

Chocolate Sandwich

DINNER

Tomato Consommé
·
Beef Wellington
Brussels Sprouts with Chestnuts   Green Salad
·
Chapel Cleeve Cold Lemon Soufflé

Mousse of Ham
·
Filet of Beef in Aspic   Winter Salad
·
Frozen Bombe

Low-Calorie Vegetable Soup
·
Lamb Chops Rouennaise
Celery, Zucchini, and Mushrooms
·
Orange Caramel

Chilled Vegetable Soup
·
Stuffed Striped Bass   Antipasto
·
Raspberry Fool

Panache
·
Baked Stuffed Red Snapper   Lyonnaise Potatoes
·
Green Salad   Cheese
·
Poached Pear Compote

Double Consommé

·

Quenelles de Brochet   Snow Peas
Green Salad

·

Chocolate Mousse

·

Cucumber Mousse

·

Saltimbocca   Green Salad

·

Toasted Almond Parfait

Double Consommé

·

French Canadian Veal   Green Salad

·

Chapel Cleeve Cold Lemon Soufflé

Iced Cucumber Soup

·

Boned, Stuffed, and Rolled Shoulder of Veal
Broccoli with Hollandaise Sauce

·

Iced Coffee Soufflé

Tomato Consommé

·

Poulet Suprême Meurice
Carrots, Celery, and Green Beans

·

Soufflé Monte Cristo

Mushrooms Vinaigrette

.

Poulet Normande
Summer Squash and Plum Tomatoes

.

Chocolate Soufflé

Salad Romano

.

Chicken 243
Green Rice   Green Salad

.

Hot Lemon Soufflé

Courgettes à la Grecque

.

Capon with Sauce Suprême
Rice   Spinach en Branche

.

Apricot Soufflé

Cream of Celery Soup

.

Boned Stuffed Turkey
Carrots, Celery, and Green Beans

.

Yorkshire Trifle

Fresh Caviar

.

Roast Saddle of Lamb
Snow Peas   Tomatoes Stuffed with Potato Purée

.

Green Salad   Cheese

.

St. John's Iced Lime Soufflé

Smoked Salmon

.

Roast Rack of Lamb
Tomatoes Provençale   Green Salad

.

Apricot Soufflé

Chick Pea Salad

.

Poached Salmon   Sauce Mousseline
Sliced Cucumbers   Vinaigrette Dressing

.

Compote of Fruits

Cheese Profiteroles

.

Bouillabaisse
French or Italian Bread   Green Salad

.

Tortoni

BUFFET

Cold Poached Salmon   Sauce Verte

.

Braised Beef
Green Rice   Winter Salad

.

Chapel Cleeve Cold Lemon Soufflé
Compote of Fruits

Nancy's Chicken   Rice
Filet of Beef in Aspic
Winter Salad

.

Iced Coffee Soufflé   Apple Tart

Smoked Salmon   Brown Bread and Butter

·

Cold Boned Stuffed Turkey
Sea Harvest   Saffron Rice
Winter Salad

·

Compote of Fruits
Chapel Cleeve Cold Lemon Soufflé
Chocolate Roll

Madras Shrimp   Condiments
Curry of Beef   Rice
Winter Salad

·

Compote of Fruits
St. John's Iced Lime Soufflé

Panache

·

Kegeree   Cottage Pie

·

Tortoni   Compote of Fruits

Virginia Baked Chicken
Potato Salad
Cold Poached Striped Bass   Sauce Verte
Antipasto

·

Orange Caramel   Toasted Almond Parfait

Chicken Breasts with Green Olives
Chick Pea Salad
Baked Stuffed Red Snapper

·

Queen's Pudding   Chocolate Mousse

Chicken 243   Green Rice
Tomato Salad
Casserole of Beef in Madeira
Salad Romano

.

Peach or Apple Tart
Eliza Fury's Essex Almond Pudding

Salmon Mousse

.

Filet of Beef in Aspic
Potato Salad   Winter Salad

.

Summer Pudding   Chocolate Sandwich

Steak, Oyster, and Kidney Pie
Cucumber Mousse   Cold Green Beans   Vinaigrette Dressing
Deviled Crab

.

Baba au Rhum   Compote of Fruits

Blanquette de Veau   Spinach Salad
Quiche Lorraine

.

Orange Caramel   Chocolate Mousse

Braised Tongue   Winter Salad
Meat Loaf de Luxe   Mushrooms Vinaigrette

.

Lemon Meringue Pie   Compote of Fruits

Blanquette de Veau   Spinach Salad
Madras Shrimp   Rice

.

Chocolate Bavarian Cream   Compote of Fruits

Veal Marengo   Green Rice
Chicken Breasts in Champagne Sauce
Tomato Salad   Vinaigrette Dressing

Chocolate Soufflé   Angel Food Cake

Shrimp Newburg   Rice
Braised Beef
Tomato Salad   Vinaigrette Dressing

Chocolate Sandwich   Poached Pear Compote

INDEX